SOUTH WEST WALES

CHILDREN'S TRAILS

D0308286

© Rebecca Lees, 2014

All Rights Reserved. No part of this publication may be reproduced, stored in a retrieval system, or transmitted in any form or by any means – electronic, mechanical, photocopying, recording, or otherwise – without prior written permission from the publisher or a licence permitting restricted copying issued by the Copyright Licensing Agency, 90 Tottenham Court Road, London W1P 0LA. This book may not be lent, resold, hired out or otherwise disposed of by trade in any form of binding or cover other than that in which it is published, without the prior consent of the publisher.

Moral Rights: The author has asserted her moral right to be identified as the Author of this Work.

Published by Sigma Leisure – an imprint of
Sigma Press, Stobart House, Pontyclerc, Penybanc Road, Ammanford, Carmarthenshire SA18 3HP.

British Library Cataloguing in Publication Data
A CIP record for this book is available from the British Library.

ISBN: 978-1-85058-998-3

Typesetting and Design by: Sigma Press, Ammanford.

Cover photograph: © Rebecca Lees top: The towpath leading to Pont Gam, Neath; below: Tenby Harbour from North Beach

Photographs: © Rebecca Lees unless stated otherwise.

Every effort has been made to fulfil requirements with regard to reproducing copyright material. The author and publisher will be glad to rectify any ommissions at the earliest opportunity

Maps: Sigma Press

Printed by: TJ International, Padstow, Cornwall

Disclaimer: the information in this book is given in good faith and is believed to be correct at the time of publication. No responsibility is accepted by either the author or publisher for errors or omissions, or for any loss or injury however caused. Only you can judge your own fitness, competence and experience. Do not rely solely on sketch maps for navigation: we strongly recommend the use of appropriate Ordnance Survey (or equivalent) maps.

SOUTH WEST WALES

CHILDREN'S TRAILS

Rebecca Lees

For Rachel & Kyffin xx

CITY AND COUNTY OF SWANSEA LIBRARIES	
6000232881	
Askews & Holts	31-Mar-2015
796.51	£8.99
OY	

Preface

If you've ever cheerfully announced to your children that you're all 'going for a walk', only to be met with moans, glum faces and sulking, then hopefully this book is for you! Its aim is to introduce children to walking in a fun, exciting way, which will hopefully inspire in them a passion for the outdoors and for exploring new places and looking for adventure.

With rising obesity levels and the associated health problems this brings, there's more need than ever to get children away from a wholly sedentary lifestyle. Research shows that more than a quarter of children in the UK are overweight or obese, with this figure rising to more than a third in Wales. And these figures are set to rise even further without change, with the National Obesity Forum predicting that more than half the UK population could be obese by 2050.

If your family has weight concerns or if you'd simply like to spend more time in the fresh air as a family, walking is an excellent activity for many reasons. In terms of getting and keeping fit, it burns calories and, if done regularly, also increases metabolism, meaning your body will burn more calories even when it's resting. It's recommended that children do at least 60 minutes of exercise every day and a good long walk – or even a number of shorter walks, such as to and from school – count towards this target, which is a great reason to start!

But there are so many more advantages to walking than just the physical benefits. There are the mental health benefits, with walking releasing lots of endorphins that quite simply make us happy! It's a great way to spend focused time together as a family and provides a good opportunity to chat about day-to-day things and important issues in a relaxed way.

It's also a brilliant way not only to teach children about nature and history as you walk, but to learn from them too! My son in particular has an amazing inability to remember what he does at school each day. Yet he clearly learns a lot because, on our walks, he is able to tell me all about things such as pine cones (or 'weather machines', as he insists they are called!), not to mention a tremendous amount about bees! He somehow forgot to tell me about the day his class was visited by beekeepers until a long walk to a honey farm prompted him to tell me far more about bees than I had ever known!

Walking also allows children to just, well, be children. I all too often find myself telling mine to calm down; to stay clean; to be careful. But on a good long walk they can get muddy, climb trees and splash in as many streams as they want, which is essential for their development, their ability to calculate risk and their connection with nature. There are some great projects around at the moment, such as the National Trust's '50 things to do before you're 11¾' and Project Wild Thing, which suggest things for children to do outdoors. Equally, they reassure parents that it's okay for children to take risks and face challenges in a safe way.

Finding time to go for walks or do any outdoor activities can be a real problem, with both parents in many families working increasingly long hours. And, in addition to being time-poor, many parents are in financially challenging circumstances and simply can't afford to pay for their children to do many outdoor activities. This isn't helped by the fact that local councils are having to take near-impossible decisions about which services to run and which to close, with the maintenance of footpaths and parks sometimes falling way down the priority list. Even whilst I was writing this book, one local authority was forced to completely scrap a planned new series of interactive children's trails due to budget cuts. It's hard to blame councils when their funding is being slashed – yet there is a clear contradiction here between the vital need to stop the ticking obesity time bomb and the simple steps that need to be taken now to actually stop it.

Then, of course, there's perhaps the hardest bit about getting children outdoors – their reluctance. Given that I've loved climbing really high mountains since I was eight, it's quite hard for me to admit that my own children aren't actually that outdoorsy. They are definitely amongst the grumblers and the face-pullers, so my trick is simply to avoid using the word 'walk' at all. Tell them you're hunting for treasure, going exploring, seeking adventure, or finding a castle; you can even resort to bribery and tell them there's an ice cream van waiting just around the next corner. Before you know it, they'll be sliding down sand dunes, traipsing through woods, sloshing through mud and generally having a brilliant time.

In our 'research' for this book, we've ticked off a fair few of the 50 Things, including rolling down lots of big hills, making mud pies, hunting for creepy crawlies, discovering what's in a pond, using a map and compass and swinging on a rope swing. Because these walks are in Wales, we've certainly done more than our fair share of running around in the rain, although we've yet to go on a night-time nature walk or set up a snail race. Luckily for my family, we still have nearly two years before my older child reaches 11¾ and I have another trails book to write!

Of course, you do need to take care and use common sense when out walking. The routes and maps in this book should be used as a guide only, and even seemingly easy walks need good preparation. Equipment such as OS maps, a compass and waterproof clothing should always be packed in your rucksack on countryside walks and walking boots or wellies worn - not flip-flops. Take extra care in bad weather and trust your own judgement, especially on trails around water, such as the trail in Chapter 2 at Stackpole. The suggested age for each trail in this book is a rough guide only, and you're the best person to decide what your child is or isn't capable of.

Some of the trails in the books are suitable for trikes and pushchairs, whilst others cover more difficult ground and are for older children rather than toddlers. Some of the trails are very short whilst others are longer and a little more challenging, but they all have plenty to see, do and talk about along the way. Where possible, I've included information on additional things to do in the area for families who want to keep exploring when the walk has finished.

I hope you and your family enjoy these trails as much as we did and that this book helps in a small way to inspire a love of walking and the great outdoors. In finding these trails and in learning about the points of interest along each, I was helped by and would like to warmly thank the following people:

My little helpers Rachel, Kyffin, Jonathan and Bethan; my big helpers Margaret and Dave Lees, Ed Jeavons, Elly Hannigan-Popp, Ken Smith, Mike May, Becky Preece, Rhian Sula, Lyndsey Maiden, Diane Berry, Lowri Jones, Kathryn Thomas, Kim Boland, Dana Thomas, Georgina Snook, Gemma Hargest, Wayne Curtis, Steve Parker and Deborah Brambley, as well as the National Trust, Ramblers Cymru, RSPB Cymru, Castle School and Stackpole School, Pembrokeshire, Clerkenhill Adventure Farm, the Wildlife Trust of South and West Wales, Carmarthenshire County Council, Neath Port Talbot County Borough Council, Glyncorrwg Ponds Visitor Centre, Margam Country Park, Afan Forest Park and the Brecon Beacons National Park Authority.

Rebecca Lees
November 2014

Contents

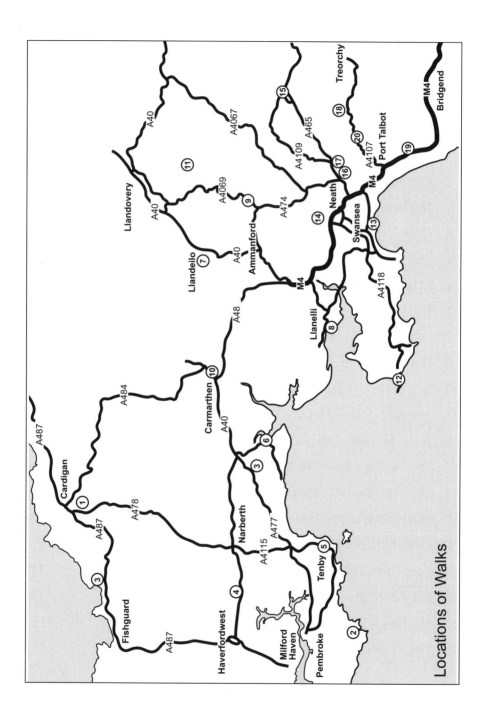

Locations of Walks

WALK 1
The Wetland Trail, Welsh Wildlife Centre, Cilgerran

There is so much at this wonderful wildlife reserve, from walking trails and cycle routes to an adventure playground and visitor centre with a spectacular glasshouse café. The trails are varied in length and scenery, with the Wetland Trail being the longest children's route within the reserve – and therefore the best for running off all that spare energy! There is also the much longer Teifi River Trail running south to Cilgerran Castle, which teenagers might enjoy but could prove too far for young children.

Approx. distance	**2 miles**
Approx. time	**1 hour**
Starting point	**Welsh Wildlife Centre, Teifi Marshes Nature Reserve**
Grading	**A level walk along tarmac and boardwalks**
Suggested age	**All ages; pushchair friendly**
Map	**OS Explorer 198**

The Wetland Trail is marked with red way-markers and follows the tarmac path anti-clockwise from the car park through the reserve's reed beds and woodland. Along the way are a number of bird hides, which can seem like great playhouses for excited children but might not be seen that way by other walkers and bird watchers! So it's important not to disturb those who come to watch the birds in peace and quiet, or the wildlife itself.

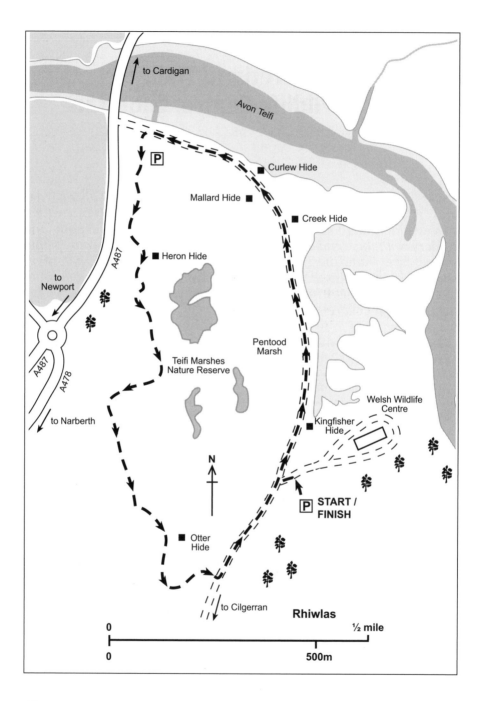

to Cardigan

Avon Teifi

P

Curlew Hide ■

Mallard Hide ■

Creek Hide ■

A487

■ Heron Hide

to Newport

to Narberth

A487

A478

Teifi Marshes Nature Reserve

Pentood Marsh

Welsh Wildlife Centre

■ Kingfisher Hide

N

P START / FINISH

■ Otter Hide

to Cilgerran

Rhiwlas

| 0 | ½ mile |
| 0 | 500m |

The first hide is the kingfisher hide. Kingfishers are striking turquoise and orange birds found at still or slow-moving water. They eat fish and water insects, searching for their prey from waterside perches and flying low over the water, and are very much worth looking out for, as they are a beautiful species.

The Wetland Trail has several hides for watching wildlife

The kingfisher hide stands on a causeway built more than 100 years ago to take the Whitland and Cardigan railway over the marshlands of the Teifi estuary. This railway embankment changed the marsh by holding back the saltwater that, for centuries, had flooded in twice a day. As a result of this division of saltwater and freshwater, the Teifi Marshes has a number of habitats where you can find many types of wildlife. Its large expanse of reeds is home to reed buntings, as well as sedge warblers arriving from Africa in the spring, and in addition to kingfishers, wagtails, dippers and insects, there's a chance you might see leaping salmon or the occasional osprey from the kingfisher hide.

Continue along the tarmac path to the Creek Hide, which is set on a raised wooden walkway to the right and has stunning views over the River Teifi. Close by on the other side of the path is the Mallard Hide, which looks inland over a small reed pool. Mallards are very common ducks with a distinctive green head and yellow bill, and there's a very good chance of seeing them on the trail, especially during winter flooding.

The path curves around to the left, towards the Curlew Hide. From here the views over the river are towards Cardigan, where the Teifi flows into the sea. Soon after the Curlew Hide, look out for a gate on the left of the path, signposted with a red way-marker. The trail leaves the tarmac path here to follows a boardwalk and, if you miss the gate and carry on alongside the river, you could end up in Cardigan!

On the boardwalk, take care of small children as the reed beds are very boggy in places. The path soon becomes a woodland trail running uphill alongside a meadow. As the path rounds the corner at the top of the slope, look out for the horses on the other side of the fence, which proved very friendly towards us!

Not far from here the path reaches a short, shallow flight of steps. To the left is the Heron Hide, from which you can look back in the direction you've just come before returning to the trail. It now starts to get a little uneven in places and a couple of sharp drops and steep steps make things tricky for push-chairs, although it's still manageable.

The trail passes a meadow and through two wooden gates to a final stretch of boardwalk. On

Boardwalk paths run through the reed beds

the hot summer's day the shade from the trees here and a cool breeze from the water comes as a big relief! At a turn in the path to the left is the Otter Hide. The best hide, with its circular walls and thatched roof, has definitely been saved until last. We didn't spot any otters, unfortunately, but had the unexpected pleasure of seeing a herd of water buffalo ambling through the water! We later discovered they are common visitors belonging to a local cheese-making farmer and are invited onto the marsh during summer months to graze and keep the vegetation down to benefit the wildlife.

Water buffalo graze on the marsh

From here it's a short stroll across the bridge and back to the car park, or to the outstanding visitor centre just a short distance further on. On the lower level is a Wildlife Trust shop and the information centre, which has engaging interactive displays not only on the reserve's wildlife but also on local history. It's interesting to find out how many products were exported all over the world from Cardigan many years ago, including slate to America, timber to Norway and fish to the

Canary Islands. Welsh people also emigrated to Australia and New Brunswick, Canada. In school holidays there are also imaginative and well-supervised craft sessions for children to get stuck into whilst parents put their feet up.

The Glasshouse Café on the upper level is stunning, with sweeping views across the Teifi and the feeling you're sitting in the treetops! It's also refreshing to have a range of healthy meals on the children's menu – as well as the prospect of a glass of wine for parents! There is indoor and balcony seating, including welcoming, squishy sofas, and a sky bridge to a picnic area overlooking the marshes.

Make sure you factor in time to visit the Cherry Grove wooden adventure playground next to the visitor centre, as well as the Tree Tops hide behind the car park, which is a great place to watch butterflies.

WALK 2
Ramble and Seek, Stackpole Estate, Pembrokeshire

The Stackpole Estate, managed by the National Trust in partnership with the Countryside Council for Wales, is a stunning nature reserve in the heart of Pembrokeshire Coast National Park. There is so much wildlife here for children to see and learn about, including otters, dragonflies and bats, as well as freshwater plants such as the renowned lilies on the estate's ponds. The National Trust runs many activities and seasonal events, including bat walks, otter spotting, guided kayaking and coasteering, whilst families are also able to cycle along the miles of paths within the estate.

Approx. distance	3 miles
Approx. time	1.5 hours
Starting point	Stackpole Outdoor Learning Centre, Old Home Farm Yard, Stackpole
Grading	A mainly level walk with some steep inclines and potentially flooded paths. Extra care is needed due to the waterside nature of this trail
Suggested age	7+
Map	OS Explorer OL36

The Ramble and Seek trail is one of a series of walks created by Ramblers Cymru in partnership with the National Trust to encourage more families to take up walking. Trail packs are available from Stackpole Outdoor Learning Centre, an eco-award winning residential centre used for educational trips, family holidays and celebrations

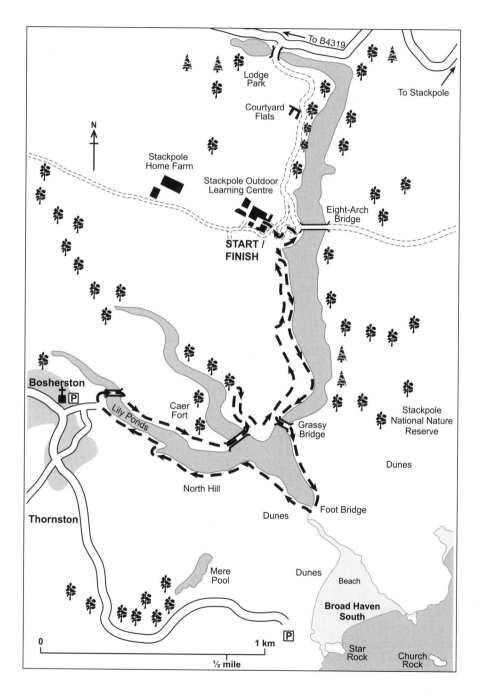

To B4319

To Stackpole

Lodge
Park

Courtyard
Flats

N

Stackpole
Home Farm

Stackpole Outdoor
Learning Centre

Eight-Arch
Bridge

START /
FINISH

Bosherston

Caer
Fort

Lily Ponds

Grassy
Bridge

Stackpole
National Nature
Reserve

Dunes

North Hill

Foot Bridge

Thornston

Dunes

Mere
Pool

Dunes

Beach

Broad Haven
South

0   1 km

½ mile

Star
Rock

Church
Rock

and a hub of activity all year round. The centre is also the starting point for this walk. The centre is not easy to find with satnav and, as the location is deep in the countryside, there's a good chance you won't pick up a mobile phone signal if you want to make enquiries on the way, so it's advisable to check the route in advance and follow the brown signs.

Alternatively, walkers can start from the National Trust car park at Bosherston Lakes, which has public toilets and a nearby pub and tearoom in the village. Bosherston comes more than halfway through the trail if starting from the Outdoor Learning Centre but, if you want to start from here, just pick up the directions further in the chapter and complete the first section last.

From the Outdoor Learning Centre, follow the track downhill towards the lake. The first sight to see is Eight-Arch Bridge, which was built more than 200 years ago and is still standing strong! Ramblers Cymru

The trail starts from the impressive Eight-Arch Bridge

19

has also created a longer trail in the series, the five-mile Rocky Roam, which crosses Eight-Arch Bridge and is an exciting coastal walk for older children, but the Ramble and Seek trail stays this side of the lake and follows the path south.

The estate grounds were designed to look beautiful but Stackpole was also a working estate, with the tracks and bridges over the lakes being created to enable the workers to go about their jobs. After about half a mile, the lakeside path crosses the Grassy Bridge, which is even older than Eight-Arch Bridge and was built as a damn to create the lake. It's not as big or impressive as Eight-Arch Bridge, but suits its surrounding perfectly. The name might suggest the bridge isn't very substantial but, as it's actually a grass-covered stone causeway, it's safer to cross than it sounds!

Grassy Bridge takes you around the lily ponds and towards the western arm of the lakes. The water on this side comes from underground springs, which can cause water levels to change dramatically between summer and winter. In fact, when we did this trail very early in 2014, this section was flooded and we had to slosh through water a few inches deep to reach the other side, so in winter wellies are essential!

The waterlilies at Bosherston are at their best in June and July, but there is so much plant and wildlife to see all year round. Peer into the water and see if you can spot the Bosherston lake pike, large fish most easily spotted from the causeways. If you are incredibly lucky you might see an otter, but these are very shy creatures and usually seen only when the estate is quiet, which is why the National Trust-led otter walks start at 7am! There are waterfowl, including diving ducks in the winter, and you might hear or even see reed warblers and water rails. There are so many more species around the lakes and in the woodland, so allow plenty of time for this walk as it might take longer than you think!

At the far end of the lily pond, look out for the first glimpse of the sea and follow the trail to the beach at Broadhaven South (which is not to be confused with a much bigger beach at Broad Haven, further west). The views from here are spectacular and it's a popular beach

Church Rock looks dramatic on a stormy day

with walkers, sunbathers and surfers. The jagged stack rising from the sea is Church Rock, which can look very dramatic on a stormy winter's day!

From Broadhaven South, take care to pick up the correct path to continue around the lily ponds. To the right, as you face the sea, is a path disappearing around the rocks. This leads to the dunes and Mere Pool, a great place to see dragonflies and damselflies. But our trail doubles back in a northerly direction, parallel to the way we came but on the other side of the pond. It's rocky and steep initially but quickly levels out to follow the nooks and crannies of the pond westwards.

Cross the small wooden bridge and climb several stone steps, passing the small fishing jetty at the water's edge. Not far past here is a ruined boiler house and a path running uphill on the left to Bosherston, which is mentioned above as an alternative starting point. It's a good place for a break as there are toilets at the car park and the tearoom and pub are good options for a hearty lunch if you haven't brought a picnic. To reach the village, go through the car park and bear left past St Martin's and All Angels Church, and then keep left along the main road.

Back at the lake, continue along the western arm, crossing the next bridge with care as it has a handrail only on one side. Follow the path right and, at the fork, keep to the path on the left, as the cliff drops rather steeply on the right. Continue down the steep steps and over another bridge before walking uphill to a T-junction. Turn left, following the 'alternative route' sign, then bear right at the top of the hill, away from the metal gate.

Bosherston Lakes are renowned for their water lilies (*Photo by Mike May*)

At the top is a vantage point across the lily ponds to Broadhaven South and Church Rock. Don't follow the narrow path straight ahead, as this leads to the cliff edge, but keep left and follow the wider path until it drops sharply downhill. It eventually re-joins the main waterside track on which the trail began, so follow this left, back to Eight-Arch Bridge and the Outdoor Learning Centre.

The Ramble and Seek trail gives wonderful waterside views almost all the way, but there is so much more to see in other parts of the estate, including the former site of Stackpole Court, the lovely Lodge Park Woods and miles of glorious coastline. These are explored in the other routes in the walking pack created by Ramblers' Cymru and the National Trust, including the Toddle Waddle, a 1.5-mile stroll through the woods for very young children. Those aged six and above can try the two-mile Wellie Wander, whilst The Rocky Roam is a challenging trek for children aged 11 and above, crossing Eight-Arch Bridge to follow the coastline from Stackpole Quay to Broadhaven South. For more information visit **www.ramblers.org.uk/wales**

WALK 3
The Nevern-ending Trail, Newport, Pembrokeshire

There are lots of secrets to uncover in Newport and its historic harbour, The Parrog – but you have to look carefully! From tales of swashbuckling sea-farers to a 5,000 year old burial chamber, there are plenty of clues to the past along this lovely trail – so many clues, in fact, that it might take quite some time to get around!

Approx. distance	2.5 miles
Approx. time	1.5 hours
Starting point	The Parrog, Newport
Grading	A mainly level walk with a short climb and some busy roads
Suggested age	5+
Map	OS ExplorerOL35

Newport lies at the mouth of the Nevern Estuary on Pembrokeshire's north coast. Although popular, it does not attract the same hoards as southern tourist spots like Tenby and Saundersfoot and the pace here is unhurried and peaceful, even during school holidays. The trail follows the Nevern upstream before exploring Newport's quaint town centre, which, although small, has plenty of attractions such as a dolls' house collection, enticing cafés and Newport Castle. The castle is privately owned and not open to visitors, but there is a lot to learn about it along the trail and it's a good focal point for little history hunters.

The Normans settled in Newport more than 1,000 years ago. Over time it grew into a busy port and ship building area, with ships bringing in cargos of lime and coal during high tide then sailing back out to far-off destinations with wool, herrings and slate. The homes along the seafront were for the ship's captains and traders, and several pubs were also clustered around the harbour.

The Parrog beach at Newport is ideal for rock pooling

The Parrog is one of Newport's two beaches, the other being Newport Sands on the other side of the estuary. The Parrog is the smaller and rockier of the two; it's lovely for rock pooling and is easily accessible from the town, but it's inadvisable to swim here due to unpredictable currents. Newport Sands is a much bigger and sandier stretch patrolled by lifeguards, with a safe swimming area clearly marked by flags.

Depending on the tide, Newport Sands can appear to be, quite literally, a stone's throw from The Parrog, but this is the point at which currents from the sea and estuary collide and it can be very dangerous to try to wade across. It's much safer to make the three-mile road trip

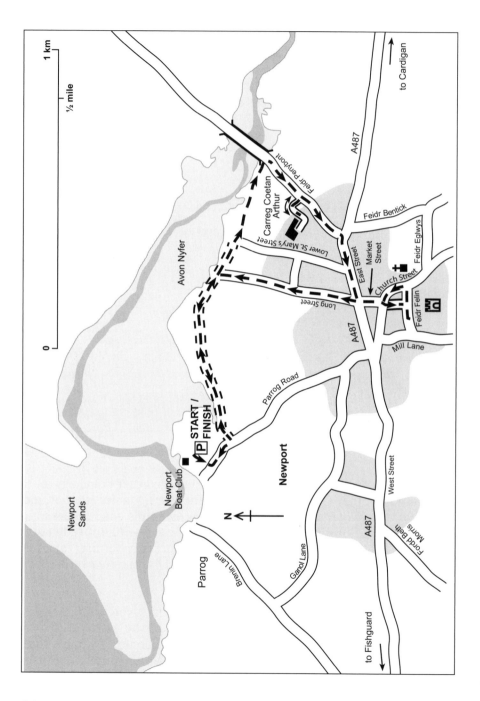

through the town and across the estuary to Newport Sands, where there's plenty of car parking, including on the beach itself.

The trail starts at Newport Boat Club at The Parrog, where there's a large public car park and toilets. From the entrance of the car park, with the boat club behind you, turn left and pick up the wide track following the estuary upstream. It's an easy access track suitable for wheelchairs and buggies and forms part of the 186-mile Pembrokeshire Coast Path, as well as the newer Wales Coastal Path, which officially opened in 2012 and is 870 miles long!

The path soon dips into woodland, continuing to run parallel to the estuary. Before long there's a lane on the right; this is the way the trail returns to the harbour later but, for now, go past the lane to the information board. It explains that the original Newport Castle was built on this spot and, if you look carefully to the left of the tennis courts, you can still see the grassy ridges and hollows in the field marking the spot on which it stood.

The Normans, who had lots of power in Britain after William the Conqueror won the Battle of Hastings, initially built a fort a few miles away at Nevern. But they later moved here as it was a good spot for spying potential enemies trying to attack from the sea. Eventually they also abandoned this castle and built a new one further up the hill, past the town – which is where we'll arrive later!

Opposite the tennis court is a short footpath to a secluded bench and a perfect picnic spot at the water's edge. Carry on along the main path for a quarter of a mile until you reach a pretty white iron bridge. If the tide is low, look out for the Pilgrim's Stepping Stones upstream of the bridge. They are said to date from medieval times, when religious people called pilgrims crossed the Nevern on their way to St David's further down the coast. The iron bridge is also a good place to look for birds, as the estuary is home to many species. Among the wading birds found here are plovers, including some that come here in winter to escape even colder countries like Scandinavia and Russia – as well as northern parts of Britain!

Go through the gate and turn right onto the road, which is called Feidr Pen y Bont. There's no pavement for a short stretch and this road can

The trail has lovely views of the Nevern Estuary

get busy in the summer as it's the way to Newport Sands, so walk carefully. Shortly on the right there's a private road, which you can't drive into unless you are a resident, but walkers are allowed. In the top right-hand corner, in the small field, is the Carreg Coetan Arthur burial chamber, which is 5,000 years old!

This type of tomb, with a number of upright stones supporting a flat horizontal stone, is known as a dolmen or, to give it its Welsh name, a cromlech. Carreg Coetan Arthur has four uprights, but only two actually support the capstone. It dates from the Neolithic Age, which is also known as the New Stone Age, but there is a bit of mystery about who was buried here!

From the burial chamber, follow your footsteps back to Feidr Pen y Bont and keep going uphill a few hundred yards until you reach the T-junction. Turn right onto East Street, which is part of the busy A487 running from Cardigan to Fishguard. On the right is Llys Meddyg. 'Meddyg' is the Welsh word for doctor and this used to be the doctor's house, but it's now a hotel. From here it's a short walk to a crossroads and you're in the hub of Newport, with a deli, an Aladdin's cave of an antiques shop and a couple of village stores.

At the crossroads turn left into Market Street, heading slightly uphill as you pass those tempting, family-friendly cafés. On the right is Ty Twt, a tiny but fascinating museum housing a private collection of dolls' houses, toys and games. It is open to the public but not every day, so check ahead for opening times if you're keen to visit.

Continue up Market Street and straight ahead into the picturesque Castle Street, where the tarmac quickly tapers into a small footpath. Follow the narrow steps to a lane called Feidr Felin and the castle is in front of you. Turn right and a short way along the lane is a small clearing, where you can peek through the gate at the castle's towering walls and imagine what it would have been like to live here hundreds of years ago (or what it's like to live here now, for that matter!).

The castle is an impressive clue to Newport's past but, if you look around, you might find some clues to the future too! In this clearing

Newport Castle sits above the town

we found lots of fallen pinecones or, as my children call them, weather machines! Collect a few and see how they look. If the pines are open, sunny weather is ahead whilst, if the pines are tucked inwards, we're in for a damp spell. On the day of our visit they were halfway in, halfway out – which pretty much sums up a Welsh summer, really!

Head back along Feidr Felin, passing the steps back to Castle Street and instead continuing towards the church at the end of the lane. There are some more good views of the castle through the hedge along this lane. The church was also originally built by the Normans, although much of the stonework you see today was added later, and in the graveyard are buried many of the sailors and shipbuilders responsible for making Newport the town it was.

From here turn left into Church Street and carry on downhill, passing the Glan Towy bakery and circling back to the top of Market Street. Walk down to the crossroads and straight ahead into Long Street, which runs gently downhill back to the coastal path past pretty holiday cottages, the local school and a skate park. Also on Long Street is Newport National Park Centre, which houses the tourist information centre and is packed with leaflets on local attractions and tide times, as well as gifts, toys and books.

At the end of Long Street, turn left onto the coastal path and make your way back to the harbour, factoring in time for a well-deserved ice cream and a spot of rock pooling – keeping an eye on that tide, of course!

WALK 4
The Spooky Wood, Clerkenhill Adventure Farm, Pembrokeshire

Of all the trails in this book, the Spooky Wood trail is undoubtedly the most extraordinary! It is the perfect example of how to get children walking without once mentioning the word 'walk'; it's simply a brilliant adventure and the fact that more than a mile is clocked up along the way is a bonus!

Approx. distance	1 mile
Approx. time	1 hour +
Starting point	Clerkenhill Adventure Farm, Slebech, Pembrokeshire
Grading	A level walk along a unique and well-planned woodland trail
Suggested age	All ages; pushchair friendly
Map	OS Explorer OL36

Clerkenhill Adventure Farm and Frisbee Golf Course, next to the main A40 road between Narberth and Haverfordwest, has, since opening ten years ago, grown from a small, quirky hideaway to one of Pembrokeshire's best days out. There's an admission charge, so unfortunately this trail isn't free, but the cost represents excellent value for money, as there are so many other things to do before and after the walk.

Be warned that the trail might take far longer than an hour to complete! There are many diversions along the way, such as rope

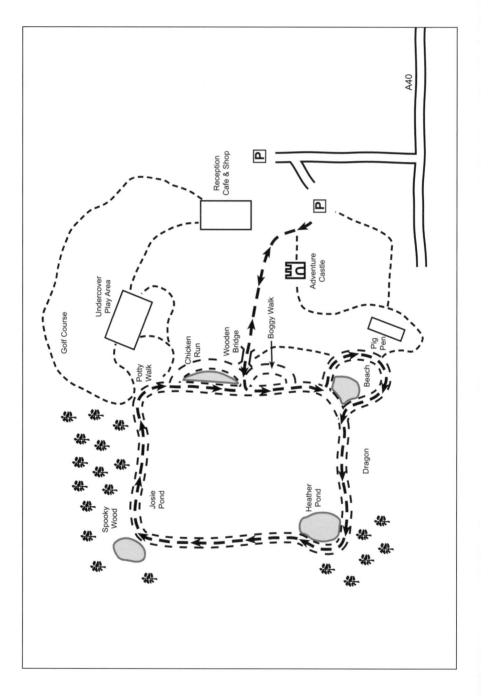

swings, wooden climbing frames and even a man-made beach, as well as many interesting (and eccentric) sculptures. Oh, and don't forget to look out for the bears and ghosts! The lovely thing about the route is that it's short enough for and manageable with toddlers, yet it's so funny and unexpected that children of ten or even older are kept entertained all the way too.

To start the Spooky Wood trail, head through the adventure playground and cross the wooden bridge between the Boggy Walk and the Chicken Run. This is where parents realise how hard it's going to be to actually get started on this trail, as instantly there's another round of giant tube tunnel slides and tree swings which children simply must try out! The trail is a simple circular (or square!) walk that is best done in a clockwise direction. It can be done in reverse, and a series of questions on wooden posts along the trail are repeated from the opposite direction, but some of the highlights are best seen from a clockwise approach.

From the starting point, head left, where the first stop is the beach. Yes, in the middle of rural Pembrokeshire you can pull up a deckchair

A lovely spot for a picnic!

and relax at a sandy cove, fully stocked with buckets and spades and next to a picturesque lily pond. But watch out, as there might be a shark or two about! As well as the humorous signs along the trail, there is also lots of interesting information about the land and wildlife, and you can find out about the oak and ash trees here. Don't forget to look out for the small boy and girl sheltering under the trees!

Next up is the Pig Walk, a quick detour around the lily pond. Here you will find Jack and Jill, who came to Clerkenhill in 2011, as well as Alfred the Giant. He looks as if he has something very serious to ponder. Read the sign next to him to find out if he is a great inventor or just plain lazy – what do you think? Don't miss the little wooden picnic table, complete with a carved bowl of fruit sitting appetisingly on the top!

Although the walk is advertised as taking about an hour, you might find that this length of time has almost passed already and the trail has barely started! Just past Alfred is a big blue slide exiting from a cosy wooden playhouse, complete with a bedroom at the back housing

Look out for the bears!

several sleeping animals. It might be some time before you can continue!

From here follow the trail out of the woods to the big red dragon, which stands in open countryside. Along the path from here children can engage with the scenery and nature by reading and answering the questions on the boards, and there's also a bird hide in which to keep a quiet lookout for interesting species. There are spectacular views of the Preseli Hills in the distance, whilst a little nearer is the landmark steeple of Slebech Church, and there are several benches and wooden tables to stop at and take it all in.

At the top left corner of the trail's 'square' is a short diversion around the heather pond, along a boardwalk. It leads to some blue slides but needs extra care as it can be slippery in wet weather and is not too stable for pushchairs, so alternatively stick to the main path.

The next things to look out for are the bears and this is where it gets scary, as brave adventurers have to creep through the bear cave to reach the woods! Here, the path forks. It converges soon after but we opted for the fork to the left and found a mini fitness trail to try out!

From here the trail arrives at Josie Pond, the oldest pond at Clerkenhill and a beautiful, peaceful place. Clerkenhill's ponds are full of natural wildlife and Josie Pond is the home of a number of jumping fish. After Josie Pond is the heart of the Spooky Wood, so don't forget to count the spooks in the trees! How many can you see? Look out for the Gruffalo, a five-eyed monster and Dai the Farmer. Scariest of all is Dai's wife, Bronwen, who might get you with her rolling pin if you don't behave!

If you can take your eyes from the ghosts and ghouls you might see some grey squirrels and other woodland creatures. There are also several varieties of tree, including the silver birch, which is common in the UK. Turn the final corner of the 'square', which leads to the Potty Walk, a jumble of ceramic pots and statues with plenty of seating areas for a rest. The Potty Walk is certainly full of surprises – but visitors should be expecting that by now!

Next to the Potty Walk is an 18-hole Frisbee golf course and nearby is an undercover play area with ride-on tractors for smaller children.

The adventure castle, with rope bridges and walkways, is an exciting recent addition and there are many animals to see and pet. One of the nicest things about Clerkenhill is that, whilst benefiting enormously from recent expansion, it remains a cosy place with a stronger sense of security than some of west Wales' larger, flagship attractions. This allows parents and carers to have a rest in relative peace on the benches and seating areas whilst children run around within earshot.

A picnic area is close to the adventure playground and there's also a new, octagonal wooden gazebo ideal for eating packed lunches under when the weather's not so good. The cosy

Deeper into the Spooky Wood

Old Loft Café is adjacent to the shop, where visitors can also buy ice creams, cold drinks and teas and coffees. It's refreshing to be served takeaway hot drinks in spotty china rather than throwaway plastic, the sight of visitors sipping from mugs adding to Clerkenhill's warm and welcoming homeliness.

WALK 5
The Tenby Trail, Pembrokeshire

If you visit Pembrokeshire, it's pretty much obligatory to go to Tenby at some point! Once there, it's easy to see why the coastal town is so well loved. It's bursting with character, is geared towards families and has more attractions and gorgeous views than you can shake a sandy spade at.

Approx. distance	5.5 miles
Approx. time	3-4 hours
Starting point	The Norton, North Beach, Tenby
Grading	A town and coastal walk with some steep cliff top sections
Suggested age	6+
Map	OS Explorer OL36

On Pembrokeshire's south coast, Tenby is easy to reach, with a train station a few minutes' walk from the beach and plenty of car parking. In the heart of Tenby is the old town, its medieval walls enclosing a maze of cobbled streets and higgledy-piggledy buildings dating back to the Norman era, as well as Tudor times when Tenby was a busy port trading goods across the channel to Europe. It is said that the first oranges to be seen in Wales arrived in Tenby!

Tenby was also extremely popular with the Georgians and Victorians, and many of the tall, colourful hotels and guest houses along the seafront were built during the town's heyday as a seaside resort. On the spot where the lifeboat station stands – which we will pass on this

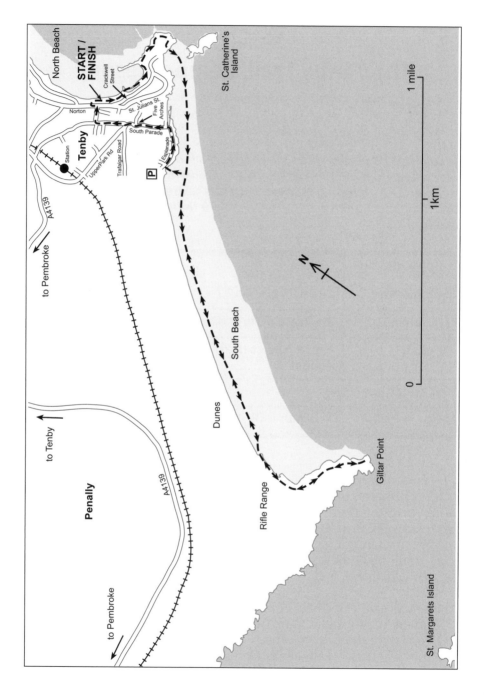

trail – there was once a grand pier, where visitors would arrive from Swansea and Bristol on steamers.

This is a long trail from Tenby town centre all the way to Giltar Point, which has exceptional views of Caldey Island and its little sister, St Margaret's island. The trail takes in the length of South Beach, which is one and a half miles long, and walking across the sand each way can really zap the energy from little legs! But the walk can easily be amended or completed in two halves, depending on how long your stay in Tenby is.

The trail starts from The Norton, the street above North Beach. A good marker to start from is the bright red letter box in front of the Cliffe Norton Hotel, from which a zig-zag path leads down to the promenade. The views are inspiring from the very start, with the golden North Beach sweeping around to the pretty harbour.

The huge rock on North Beach is called Goskar Rock, a name given by the Vikings when they landed here more than 1,000 years ago. It's

Tenby's pretty harbour from North Beach

isolated by the sea when the tide is in but, at low tide, it sits on the middle of the beach and is a magnet for low-level scrambling.

Follow the promenade right, towards the harbour, passing Tenby Inshore Lifeboat Station and a small dock. You can walk along the wall on either side of the dock but there are no railings, so keep hold of young children. Cross the courtyard and join the road, passing the tiny St Julian's Church on the harbour's edge. St Julian's is known as 'the fisherman's church' because it was built for seafarers and is made from stone brought over from Caldey Island.

On the opposite side of the road to St Julian's is a series of arches set into the curved wall. These arches once supported a road made by a rich man called Sir William Paxton. He was from Carmarthenshire, where he built a famous monument called Paxton's Tower, thought to be in memory of Lord Nelson.

Follow the road uphill past the arches. This hill is called Penniless Cove Hill! Walk past the Caldey Island boat trip kiosks and follow Castle Square to Laston House, which has a blue plaque on the wall and was also built by Paxton.

Laston House was built more than 200 years ago and was designed with indoor sea water swimming pools, built especially for rich tourists who wanted to enjoy the water whatever the weather! Many years ago, it was thought that sea water was a cure for all kinds of ailments, and it was very fashionable to visit a seaside resort to 'take the waters'. Walking along the promenade was also a very popular activity – but this was as much to do with being seen by important people as it was about keeping fit! Laston House was also the site of Tenby's assembly rooms, which again was a focal point for rich people to be seen, meet friends, drink tea and coffee and catch up with the gossip of the day.

Continue along the path until, just around the corner, the old lifeboat station comes into view. The red and grey building is certainly very striking, but would you want to live in it? Well, believe it or not, the station is now a home! Taken out of use in 2005, 101 years after it was built, it was saved from demolition and renovated by a private developer. His struggle to convert the building was documented on Channel 4's *Grand Designs* programme, which showed the difficulty in getting materials to the precarious site and engineers racing to finish certain jobs before the tide came in!

The old lifeboat station is now someone's home!

Shortly past the old lifeboat station, the path forks. To visit the new station and to walk around the base of Castle Hill, continue to the left. The best views, however, are gained by climbing the hill, bearing right and then left to the top. The views from here include a bird's eye perspective of the new lifeboat station, the shape of which, to us, resembled an admiral's hat like the one Lord Nelson wore!

Tenby's Welsh name is Dinbych y Pysgod, which translates as 'the little fort of fishes', and Castle Hill is thought to have been the site of an Iron Age settlement. When the Normans arrived in Britain, they invaded West Wales and built their own castle on the top of this hill, which has the best view of enemies approaching from the sea. The ruins of a medieval tower remain and Tenby Museum and Art Gallery stands on the site of the castle's living quarters.

The museum itself is particularly interesting and, even if you don't have time for a visit, make sure to take a look at the beautiful blue mosaic exterior wall. Also on Castle Hill is the Welsh memorial to Prince Albert, who was Queen Victoria's husband and is said to have brought the tradition of Christmas trees to Britain.

Castle Hill overlooks St Catherine's island and its fort, which was built as a lookout at the time a French invasion was feared. This tiny island, which is just 100m from the mainland, also once housed a zoo! It's possible to reach the island at low tide but visitors must take care not to get cut off by the sea and become stranded. The bandstand overlooking St Catherine's island is not the original, which was made to celebrate Queen Victoria's diamond jubilee in 1897. This was dismantled during World War II because the metal was needed for the war effort, and the stand here today is a replica built in 1991.

St Catherine's fort from Castle Hill

Head down to the bandstand and take the steps on the right to Castle Beach. This is the start of the trek across the sand until you reach the dunes in the distance! As you start walking across Castle Beach, take a look at the gardens and terraces set into the cliff, and yet more rows of painted Georgian townhouses enjoying enviable views high above the beach.

Castle Beach is the smallest of Tenby's beaches and in low tide you can walk from it straight onto South Beach. This has a safe swimming area marked by flags, after which the beach becomes less crowded, tending to attract dog walkers rather than sunbathers. If the tide is in, making the beach inaccessible, a parallel path runs past the golf course on the other side of the burrows.

At the far end of the beach are the remains of some old walls and, beyond these, the Pembrokeshire Coast Path is signposted with an acorn symbol. This is a 186-mile trail running from St Dogmael's near Cardigan to Amroth, seven miles beyond Tenby. Since 2012 it's also been part of the Wales Coastal Path and the stretch between Tenby and Lydstep is very popular with long-distance and day hikers.

It's essential to note that the dunes area between Giltar Point and the village of Penally is an MoD firing range and, on the days it's in use, red flags will fly to warn walkers to stay away. You can also find out firing times in advance by visiting the UK government website. If the firing range is not in use, follow the coastal path steps to the cliff top and continue left across the dunes towards Giltar Point.

It is possible to scramble right out to the head of Giltar Point along a narrow, rocky 'neck'. The path is well defined but it's not for the faint-hearted and you will need to supervise children closely. From the Point, Caldey Island appears almost within touching distance and, if you are not making the boat trip to the island, this is the best spot from which to see it.

Caldey is a small island just one and a half miles long and one mile wide. It's made up of Caldey and 'little Caldey', otherwise known as St Margaret's island, which becomes cut off from the main island at high tide. Caldey is home to and owned by Cistercian monks and is open to visitors between Easter and October. Boat trips run from the harbour or Castle Beach, depending on the tide, and tickets can be bought from the kiosks at Castle Square.

The cost of the boat trip and admission to the island is £11 for adults, £10 for concessions and £6 for children (2014). This might seem expensive for a family but Caldey is a unique attraction with plenty to fill a day, including walking trails, the sandy Priory Beach, chanted services in the abbey church and the chance to buy perfume, chocolate and shortbread made by the monks. There is also a village Post Office, where visitors can buy and post cards franked with a special Caldey hand stamp.

When you're ready, retrace your steps back along the coastal path and along South Beach. Instead of continuing back to Castle Beach, leave South Beach just beyond the lifeguard station, passing the new South Beach Shack complex, where ice-cream, tea, coffee and takeaway food is sold and there's also a bar and grille. Follow the paved zig-zags uphill to the Esplanade. To the left is a large children's play area –

although little ones might have no energy left for playing after such a long walk!

Follow the Esplanade towards the town until it turns left, past the bright blue Esplanade Hotel, into South Parade. The trail is now on the outside of the town walls, which were built by the Normans to keep out the Welsh! You'll soon see the south west gate jutting out imposingly. This is known locally as 'Five Arches' – although there are actually six arches including the one leading through the town wall!

Opposite the Five Arches is the Pembrokeshire Coast National Park Centre, which is full of leaflets and books on further things to do in Tenby and Pembrokeshire. From the arches, continue along South Parade to the junction and turn right into White Lion Street. This leads to the seafront and back to The Norton on the left.

The Five Arches leads through Tenby's medieval walls

Many of Pembrokeshire's most popular attractions are near Tenby, including Folly Farm, Tenby Dinosaur Park and Heatherton, where activities include paintballing, go-karting, pistol-shooting and zorbing. The neighbouring coastal town of Saundersfoot is also a favourite for tourists and you can even walk there from Tenby along the coastal path – but that's another trail altogether!

WALK 6
Dylan Thomas Centenary Walk, Carmarthenshire

A trail around Laugharne really had to be included in this book because 2014 marks the centenary of the man who put the pretty seaside town on the map. Welsh poet and playwright Dylan Thomas, famous for his play Under Milk Wood and his many poems, as well as children's story A Child's Christmas in Wales, was born 100 years ago in Swansea. His family, however, came from Carmarthenshire and he spent many childhood holidays in Laugharne before settling here with his wife Caitlin and their own children.

Dylan died at the young age of 39 whilst in New York in 1953, but for the last years of his life the family lived at the Boat House on the edge of the Taf estuary, where Dylan had inspiring views over the water from his writing shed, a stone's throw from his home.

Approx. distance	2.5 miles
Approx. time	1.5 hours
Starting point	Laugharne town square cark park
Grading	A town, coastal and countryside trail with a steep hill and muddy sections. Not suitable for pushchairs
Suggested age	5+
Map	OS Explorer 164

Laugharne remains a quiet, unspoilt town, although it does get busy in the height of summer! It's celebrating the centenary of Dylan's birth

The Boat House was Dylan Thomas' home in Laugharne

with a number of events, whilst this trail is based on Dylan's own celebration of his 30th birthday on 27th October, 1944. To mark the day he took a walk from the town to St John's Hill and afterwards wrote a poem, called *Poem in October*, about his love of Laugharne and his thoughts on getting older. The route Dylan took has now been made into the Birthday Walk route, marked by a series of brown signs and inscriptions. Our trail follows the Birthday Walk for some of the way but is longer, to take in more of the countryside and some interesting places in the town connected to Dylan.

The car park lies next to the A4066, to the left of the town square and in front of the castle. Be aware that it's a tidal car park and can flood on occasion! Running alongside the car park is the River Coran and beyond that is the Taf estuary, stretching to the sea. On the far side of the estuary is Llansteffan, where Dylan had friends and would visit regularly.

From the car park, cross the small humpback bridge and follow the path below the castle, overlooking the estuary. As you round the castle, look for the brown sign on the left pointing to the Dylan Thomas Boat House. Leave the estuary path to follow the footpath as it runs uphill alongside the castle and past two cottages. The lane bears left then quickly right, past a large house called Sea View. Dylan and Caitlin lived here during their earlier years in Laugharne and Caitlin once described it as the happiest time of their lives.

Join Victoria Street at the end of the lane and head right, past the graveyard. At the caravan park another brown Boat House sign points right and soon the path is running above the Taf, giving lovely views. Shortly on the left are some steps leading to a bird hide, which is worth climbing up to as the view opens up even further the higher you are. From this spot you can look back over the route you have just taken and see St John's Hill beyond the castle. Called Bryn Sir John in Welsh, this is where Dylan walked on his 30th birthday.

Rejoin the path, which is part of the Carmarthen Bay Coastal Path and the relatively new Wales Coastal Path. From here it's only a short distance to Dylan's writing shed and then the Boat House itself. The writing shed, painted a cheerful sea green, is on the right. Take a peek inside and see what it would have been like sitting at the writing desk,

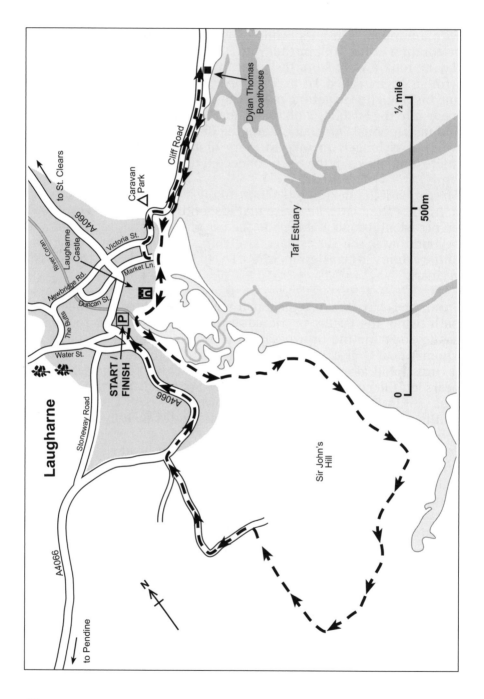

Laugharne

to St. Clears

A4066

River Corran

Laugharne Castle

Newbridge Rd.

Victoria St.

Market Ln.

The Butts

Duncan St.

Water St.

Stoneway Road

A4066

to Pendine

START / FINISH

P

Caravan Park

Cliff Road

Dylan Thomas Boathouse

Taf Estuary

Sir John's Hill

N

½ mile

500m

0

overlooking the sea and listening to the gulls. It doesn't look as if Dylan was particularly tidy!

A short distance past the shed is a gate in the wall and steps leading down to the Boat House. This is where Thomas lived for the last four years of his life with Caitlin and their sons Llewelyn and Colm and daughter Aeronwy. A plaque commemorating Aeronwy can be seen in the front garden. Today the Boat House is a museum and tearooms.

Dylan's writing shed, overlooking the Taf Estuary

There is a small charge to look around the museum and children under seven can go in for free.

Follow the path back to the writing shed and step over the low stone stile onto the steps down to the beach, taking care as they are very steep and uneven. The beach here is not sandy but extremely squelchy and muddy, whilst the rocks are seaweed-strewn and treacherously slippery, so it's definitely best to keep to the stone causeway! Follow the causeway back towards the castle, passing a wooden shelter and a series of inscriptions from Dylan's work as you go.

The trail has a 'figure of eight' shape and this is the point it reaches the car park again and passes through it into the second loop of the 'eight'. Walk to the furthest end of the car park from the castle where, beyond the metal barrier, our trail picks up the Birthday Walk and follows it towards St John's Hill. The Taf runs parallel to the path on the left and it's again worth noting that banks of the estuary are very muddy and the tide can come in quickly, so it's advisable to stay on the path.

Follow the Birthday Walk uphill into the woodland. During the climb, look back towards Laugharne Castle as there are again great views from higher ground. Castell Talacharn, as it is in Welsh, was built from earth and timber by the Normans in 1116. The Normans came from France and took power in England, gradually inching their way into

Wales too. The Welsh weren't happy about their town being taken over and so attacked and captured the castle several times!

The parts of the castle you can see today are 500-600 years old and a powerful landowner called Sir John Perrot lived here in Tudor times. He was a firm friend of Queen Elizabeth I but eventually fell out of her favour and was found guilty of plotting against her, which was treason! He was locked up in the Tower of London and died before it was decided whether he should be executed or not!

Follow the path until you reach a short flight of wooden steps and go through a gate into Salt Marsh Farm. This section is still part of the Birthday Walk and is also known as the 'New Walk', which was made more than 150 years ago for cocklers. Their job was to collect small clams called cockles from the beach but, when high tides blocked the cart track, they couldn't get to work, so the footpath was created as an alternative.

Approximately a quarter of a mile from the gate, the woodland opens out to the left, giving beautiful views over the burrows and Carmarthen Bay. You can also see all the way back to the Boat House in the direction from which you've just come. Keeping right, continue through the woodland, following the small white circular signs way-marking Laugharne via St John's Hill. For half a mile the path rises and falls, the burrows beneath gradually changing into green fields.

The path reaches a fork, descending to the left and climbing to the right. Take the right fork uphill, heading away from the sea, and climb a flight of very steep wooden steps – almost a ladder! - to a stile. Continue uphill to a second stile, which brings you into an open field. Cross the field, keeping to the left to begin with then gradually bearing towards the centre of the hedge running along the top of the field. Head for the metal gate in the hedge and cross the stone stile next to it into another field.

Cross this field bearing slightly right of the centre (towards one o'clock), with the farmhouse on the right. Climb over another stile and leave the field, joining the tarmac lane and turning left as it drops steeply downhill. At the bottom of the hill, continue straight ahead to rejoin the A4066 and turn right towards the town. There is a

A statue of Dylan Thomas in the centre of Laugharne

pavement until the sharp bend, where walkers have to step onto the road for a short distance before pavement picks up again. Continue past Frogmore Gardens and the Boathouse B&B to the statue of Dylan Thomas, which overlooks the estuary and the car park from which the trail started.

Dylan and Caitlin Thomas were buried at St Martin's Church in Laugharne, their grave marked by a simple white cross. A detour to the churchyard can be incorporated into this trail and there are many more places in the town and throughout Carmarthenshire that played an important part in Dylan's life. To find out more visit **www.discovercarmarthenshire.com**

WALK 7
The Castle Trail, Dinefwr, Llandeilo

Dinefwr, with its open parkland, wonderful wildlife and layers of history, is an inspiring place for young imaginations to run riot. The estate is run by the National Trust and therefore a brilliant location to have a go at some of the Trust's 50 Things to Do Before You're 11¾, such as climbing a big hill and finding your way with a map.

Approx. distance	2 miles
Approx. time	1 hour
Starting point	Dinefwr Park, Llandeilo
Grading	An uphill walk through woodland and along parkland paths
Suggested age	5+
Map	OS Explorer OL12

The park and woodland are picturesque all year round but look particularly spectacular in May, when the bluebells transform Castle Woods into an enchanting setting. The parkland also looks beautiful in October and November, when the leaves turn to orange and red and cover the paths. An autumn walk at Dinefwr is a firm favourite of our family, and we've wondered if the Trust should extend its 'things to do' list to include picking up armfuls of colourful leaves and showering yourself in them!

The trail has two 'castles', both very different in style and purpose and illustrating the changing role of Dinefwr over the centuries. The first is a 12th[h] century Welsh stronghold, reinforced by one of Wales' most powerful characters to protect the land. Admittedly the other,

Newton House, is not really a castle at all, but the turrets of this sumptuous former residence of the wealthy Rice family certainly give it a stately appearance that contrasts nicely with the medieval ruins on the hill. Life at Newton House would have been very formal in its heyday but now it's a hands-on place where young visitors can to experience what life would have been like more than 100 years ago, carrying out tasks in the servants' quarter such as polishing shoes or playing the piano in the dining room.

Note that there's a charge for non-National Trust members to use the car park and visit Newton House. The hut where visitors pay is also packed with information on Dinefwr and the National Trust and has a series of leaflets of alternative walks around the parkland. These range from short, mainly level walks that are suitable for all abilities to longer hikes such as the River Walk, which follows the path of the River Twyi and passes features including the pump house, which powered water for the whole estate, and a project area where Trust volunteers are carrying out a study of tree sparrows, a breed of farmland bird that is declining.

Dinefwr Castle is almost 1,000 years old!

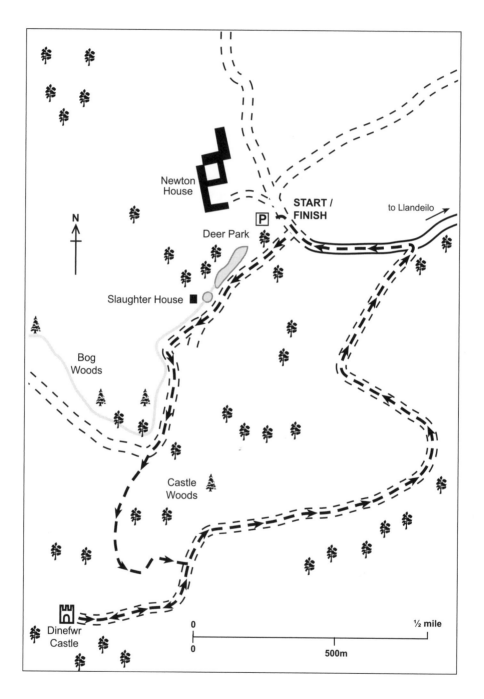

Newton House

N

Deer Park

START / FINISH

P

to Llandeilo

Slaughter House

Bog Woods

Castle Woods

Dinefwr Castle

0

0

½ mile

500m

54

Newton House is short walk from Dinefwr Castle

The Castle Walk starts from the car park. Facing away from Newton House, follow the path to the right, in the direction of the castle ruins on the hilltop. Take care over the cattle grid and follow the track towards the woodland. To the right is the deer park, which is a Site of Special Scientific Interest and home to more than 100 fallow deer. The deer park is open between certain times but the gate is locked each evening, so do read the times on the notice if you are going to go in!

The trail bears downhill and curves slightly left past a red brick lodge, which used to be the gamekeeper's cottage. It's called Mynachdy, the reason for which is a bit of a mystery as Mynachdy is Welsh for monastery. Next, on the right, is the Slaughter House, a reminder that the meat eaten by the Rice family and their workers would have been killed and prepared on the estate. It's now used for National Trust activities but has kept a lot of its old character and the winches used for lifting animals can still be seen inside the door.

Continue through the gate and then through a second gate, which is where the hard work begins! It's a pretty steep climb to the castle from here - but that was the point when its position was chosen! Castles tended to be built high up, not only for those inside to see the approaching enemy but also to make things difficult for invaders trying to get in. They would be worn out from the climb before the fighting had even begun!

About halfway up the hill, on the left hand side, pass through the gate into Castle Woods Nature Reserve. The woodland is owned by the Wildlife Trust of South and West Wales and is home to many birds, including nuthatches, woodpeckers, treecreepers and warblers. In the 1970s this beautiful woodland was set to be destroyed but was saved by a Scottish forester called Ian Watt, who had come to live in Llandeilo and who launched a fundraising campaign to create a nature reserve.

Enough money was raised to buy the woodlands, including the castle, which was covered in ivy at the time, as well as a decaying church on the estate. It's quite unusual for the Wildlife Trust to own a castle! Renovations have made it safe and now, thanks to Mr Watts' efforts,

Having a rest in Castle Woods

Castle Woods and Dinefwr Castle are accessible to everyone and free to enter. The woods have become an integral part of community activity and education and you'll see a number of attractive benches carved by local youngsters amongst the trees. If you lift the lid of the wooden information table, you'll be able to find out more.

Follow the path uphill through the wood until reaching a wider path running across the top. Follow this to the right, past another carved bench, and walk the short distance to the castle. On the final stretch uphill are several hollow trees; long-term decay causes the hollows but these make safe homes for animals and birds, including owls, bats and even foxes.

Dinefwr Castle is an impressive sight. It's now a ruin but its walls remain solid and imposing enough for visitors today to see how difficult it would have been to attack almost 1,000 years ago. That's if invaders could cross the massive ditch in the first place! The earliest known history of Dinefwr Castle is when it was in the hands of the great Welsh leader Lord Rhys, who ruled this part of Wales. It was later abandoned and fell into ruin but has remained a vital part of the landscape. The views of the River Twyi from here are stunning and the castle looks across miles of countryside, as well as itself being seen from miles around.

Although owned by the Wildlife Trust, the castle is managed by heritage group Cadw. There are battlements, staircases and secret corners to explore, and the climb to the top of the keep is worth the effort for the bird's eye view of the landscaped park. It might take some time to set off again on the trail, as there is so much scope here for children to create their own adventures!

To return, start downhill the way you came but, instead of turning back into the woods, continue along the track towards the parkland, looking out for more deer as you walk. The best times to see them are early in the morning and in the evening, as deer are shy creatures that tend to venture out when the park is quieter.

As the path comes out from the trees and circles the parkland, the turrets of Newton House come into view on the left. The track cuts across the parkland and in autumn and winter can get quite waterlogged, making it ideal for splashing in puddles in wellies! The track eventually reaches the drive, where walkers can turn left and wind their way back towards the car park and Newton House.

People have lived at Dinefwr for more than 2,000 years. Under the parkland, evidence of two Roman forts has been found, as well as a town created by Edward I about 700 years ago! An earlier manor once stood here but it was replaced by Newton House the mid-1600s, with the turrets and other improvements being added later. There is lots for children to see and do inside, including 'Hidden House' tours describing how the servants lived and worked, and there is also a lovely tearoom in what used to be the billiard and smoking room.

Several outbuildings would have been needed to make sure a house and estate the size of Dinefwr ran smoothly. If you have time after the trail, explore the grounds and take a look at the ice house, which was a much-needed storage building in the days before fridges and freezers were invented! There are also formal gardens behind Newton House and many family activities are held in the parkland throughout the year, including bug hunts, wildlife tracking events and tractor trailer tours for visitors wanting to find out more about the ancient breed of white cattle living on the land.

Dinefwr Park is on the edge of Llandeilo, a pretty town known for its distinctive rows of painted houses. It has several cafés, shops, an ice cream parlour and free parking, giving easy access into Dinefwr Park. Discover Carmarthenshire has a series of town and countryside trails, including a Llandeilo walk starting at St Teilo's Church and running through the parkland to Dinefwr Castle. It's a good way to make the most of both the town and the park in one visit and is suitable for older children, but the parkland is extensive and might prove too far for younger walkers.

WALK 8
Millennium Coastal Park, Llanelli

The 10-mile, traffic-free Millennium Coastal Park along the Loughor Estuary has transformed this former industrial area into a haven for families in search of the great outdoors. With stunning views of the Gower peninsula in one direction and towards Pembrey and Cefn Sidan beach in the other, this regenerated coastline has all the space you could want to walk, cycle, skate or scoot, as well as many superb attractions along the way.

Approx. distance	3 miles
Approx. time	1½ hours
Starting point	The Discovery Centre, North Dock, Llanelli
Grading	A mainly level trail along tarmac and footpaths
Suggested age	All ages; pushchair friendly
Map	OS Explorer 178

The coastal path as a whole runs from the Bynea Gateway to Pembrey Country Park. This trail comprises a short section in the middle, alongside Llanelli Beach and around the tranquil Sandy Water Park. It starts at the Discovery Centre in North Dock, a modern, landmark building rising in a series of decks, which make the most of the far-reaching views. The adjacent car park is very reasonably priced, although it can fill up very quickly in good weather.

From the Discovery Centre follow the path right, with the sea on your left hand side. There are plenty of benches along the way, as well as some interesting artwork. The path heads towards a small hill, which has been said by some little walkers to resemble the hill in

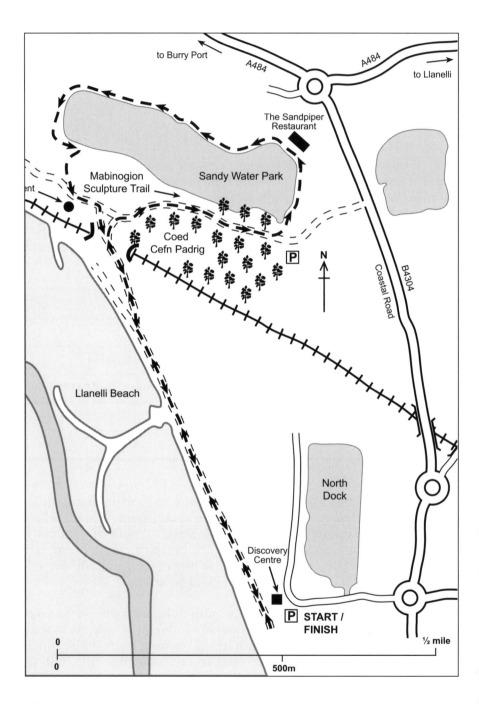

to Burry Port

A484

A484

to Llanelli

The Sandpiper
Restaurant

Sandy Water Park

Mabinogion
Sculpture Trail

ent

Coed
Cefn Padrig

P

N

Coastal Road

B4304

Llanelli Beach

North
Dock

Discovery
Centre

P START /
FINISH

0

0

500m

½ mile

Waving at trains from the Millennium Coastal Park

Teletubbyland! Follow the red path up the hill towards the obelisk at the top. You are now standing on top of a railway tunnel! This is the main line between Swansea and Pembrokeshire, with trains zipping through every 10 or 15 minutes. Find out if you are faster than a diesel train by waiting on one side of the hill for a train then racing across the top in a bid to reach the other side before the train comes out of the tunnel!

From the obelisk follow the path down the other side of the hill. Ahead is another small hillock with a stone monument on top marking Sandy Water Park, which is beyond. The trail follows the perimeter of the lake but first is a short detour through the small wood to the right. This is Coed Cefn Padrig, and a tall wooden post on the edge of the trees marks the Mabinogion Sculpture Trail.

The trail was originally created with locally-made sculptures of animals from the Mabinogion, a series of ancient Welsh folk tales. Sadly, we found that most of the sculptures have now been removed, although a wild boar, made from recycled metal, remains in a clearing towards the end of the woodland path. The detour is still worth making, however, for the wood is an exciting place for children to explore and is a haven for many types of birds and butterflies.

A wild boar on the Mabinogion Sculpture Trail

The path emerges from Coed Cefn Padrig in front of a small car park, which can make an alternative starting point for families simply wanting a short stroll around the lake. Circle the car park and cross the tarmac path to reach the railings in front of the lake then follow the paved path anti-clockwise in the direction of the Sandpiper pub and restaurant. The sloping jetties just this side of the pub are ideal places to pause and watch the swans before carrying on around the lake.

The Sandpiper is a popular family venue, with an outdoor play area and plenty of garden tables overlooking the water. Just past here the path changes from paving to fine gravel, although it is still smooth enough for pushchairs and scooters. When you have walked about halfway along this shore, look across the lake and see if you can spot the red rugby posts. It looks like a player is about to score a try between them!

The lake is pretty and peaceful now but the land looked very different until about 30 years ago, as it was the site of a huge steel works. At first it was called the Llanelly Steel Works and the name was later changed to Duport. During the early years of the Llanelly Steel Works, rates of pay were so good that it was known locally as the Klondike, after the Klondike gold rush in Canada!

The trail reaches the top shore of the lake and leaves the gravel path, crossing the wooden bridge. Continue anti-clockwise along the water's edge then fork right towards the rugby posts. Look out for the saucepans at the top of them! Llanelli used to be one of the UK's biggest producers of enamel saucepans, which gave the town the nickname 'sosbans', the Welsh word for saucepans. You might have heard a song called *Sosban Fach*, which is sung by fans of both Llanelli RFC and the Scarlets regional team. Take a look at the No. 10 in the red jersey as you walk past. He looks quite like former Llanelli fly half Phil Bennett but, as Llanelli also had another brilliant No. 10 called Jonathan Davies, it's hard to say who it might be!

Carry on straight ahead to the top of the small hillock, which brings you back to the railway line behind the safety of a high fence. The railway tunnel is on the left. Make your way to the top and then walk back along the coastal path to the Discovery Centre. Highly recommended is the first floor café, where you can tuck into a main meal or teas, coffees and ice creams whilst enjoying the views over the estuary. On the ground floor are a small shop, toilets and an information centre, whilst local groups often sell craft or display their work in the foyer.

Skimming stones at Sandy Water Park

Tide tables are also available at the centre and there's an ice cream kiosk, separate to the café, outside. There's also a bike hire scheme, as the coastal path incorporates a stretch of National Cycle Network Route 4, and nearby are a number of other great tourist attractions. Very popular is the Llanelli Wetland Centre, where you can see dragonflies, water voles, geese and flamingos, whilst Pembrey Country Park in the opposite direction has skiing, tobogganing, acres of countryside and renowned golden beaches.

WALK 9
The Secret Trail, Ynys Dawela Nature Park, Brynamman

Ynys Dawela Nature Park is the place to come to when you quite literally want to get away from it all. If your idea of a perfect day out with children includes refreshment kiosks, hustle and bustle and the knowledge there are public loos along the route, this really isn't for you. If, however, you want to bring your children to a secret wilderness where they can explore hidden corners and get right into the thick of nature, this lovely park on the brink of the Black Mountain should go to the top of your 'must visit' list.

Approx. distance	2 miles
Approx. time	1 hour
Starting point	Llandeilo Road, Brynamman
Grading	A woodland and meadow walk with some steep, uneven sections
Suggested age	4+
Map	OS Explorer OL12

Ynys Dawela Nature Park is relatively small but, as one of Carmarthenshire's lesser-visited parks, it's possible that you'll have the entire place to yourselves or at the very least meet only a handful of other visitors along your walk. It's on the outskirts of the small town of Brynamman, a largely Welsh-speaking town on the boundary of Carmarthenshire. Upper Brynamman and Lower Brynamman are separated by the River Amman, which runs along the southern perimeter of Ynys Dawela.

Ynys Dawela Nature Park

The park is an appealing patchwork of meadow, marsh, woodland and water, with a variety of creatures living here and many species of flower and plant to look out for on the trail. Interestingly, the land used to look very different to how it looks today. Ynys Dawela takes its name from an old farm that used to exist here. Parish records show that nearly 200 years ago the farmer was a man called David Jones and, in David's time, there was very little woodland, with the hillside being more open than it is now.

There are three main access points into Ynys Dawela, the best being from Llandeilo Road. Follow Station Road through Brynamman and take the sharp turn into Llandeilo Road at the Post Office. Follow the road until the houses peter out and a country lane opens up. Look for the nature reserve board on the left hand side of the lane, next to the five-bar gate, and park in the small lay-by just before it, taking care not to block the smaller gate into a field.

There is now no parking within the park itself, so the trail starts here! Pass through the five-bar gate next to the nature board and follow the

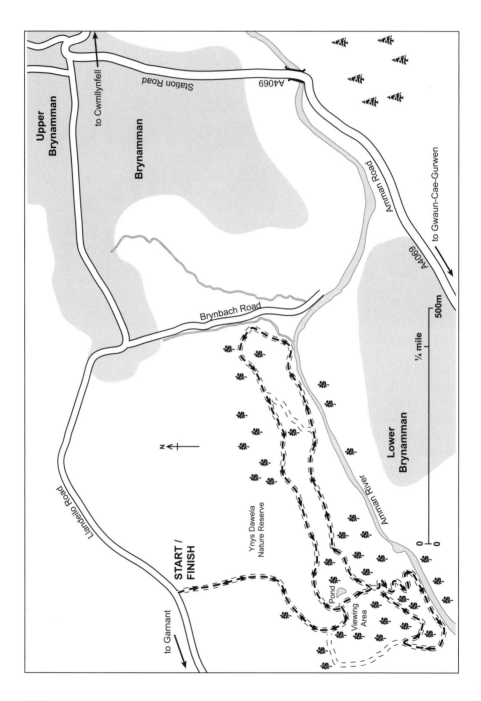

Upper Brynamman

Brynamman

to Cwmllynfell

Station Road

A4069

Amman Road

to Gwaun-Cae-Gurwen

A4069

Brynbach Road

Llandeilo Road

N

500m

¼ mile

Lower Brynamman

Amman River

START / FINISH

Ynys Dawela Nature Reserve

Pond

Viewing Area

to Garnant

wide track downhill on the edge of a grazing field for horses and cattle. From the top of the field are views across Cwm Aman to the turbines of Mynydd y Betws wind farm, which started working in 2013.

The track dips into woodland and about a third of a mile from the road is a disused car parking area, and the start of the trail proper. Ynys Dawela's small pond is on the other side of the car park and is home to dragonflies and damselflies, as well as being a spawning ground for toads, frogs and newts.

Around the pond, a number of wooden signposts point to the various trails within the nature park. They are all fairly short so this trail incorporates the Riverside Walk and the Meadow Walk, in order to cover as much of the park as possible. From the pond, walk past the large wooden shelter on the right to a three-way 'fork' in the trail.

A wide track leads left and a thin, grassy path goes to the right, whilst straight ahead is a woodland path. Follow this path straight ahead as it descends to the river, becoming steeper as it zig-zags towards the bottom. The path here is a mixture of earth and gravel that can dry out during warm weather and become easy to skid on, so take care.

Reaching the riverbank, turn right and follow the direction of the river. Not too far from here is Brynamman's outdoor swimming pool and on a still day the

The riverside trail is very secluded

faint shouts of children playing there are carried across the water. So quiet was Ynys Dawela on the day of our visit that this distant noise was the only evidence of other people we heard all afternoon!

At the metal circular gate the path turns away from the river and begins to climb back uphill through the woodland. The colours along the trail in spring are wonderful, the vibrant bluebells along the riverbank making way for the brilliant yellow of the gorse running uphill alongside the path. There are also plenty of buttercups and forget-me-nots in this part of the wood.

At the fork, take the path to the right, which bears downhill ever so slightly before curving left and continuing uphill. The trail soon returns to the three-way fork we arrived at earlier, which forms the middle of this figure-of-eight trail. This time follow the wide track of Meadow Walk, which is now straight ahead.

From here the path runs parallel with and slightly higher than the river, with glimpses of the water, as well as intermittent views of the mountainside, through the trees. On the left, the woodland opens up into meadow, which is ideal for picnics and especially pretty in summer when the flowers are in bloom.

The park is on the edge of a coalfield where, many years ago, miners dug deep underground to reach a type of coal called anthracite. The mine was abandoned a long time ago and now nature has taken back the land, with tiny mammals such as wood mice and voles sharing the hedgerows and woodland with squirrels, hedgehogs and bats.

Shortly past the meadow, a narrower path to the left can be taken as a short cut if needed, reaching a higher path and circling back to the pond. Otherwise, carry on until you reach a wooden bridge crossing a tributary stream feeding the river. Our trail doesn't cross this bridge but it's a nice spot for a quick game of Pooh Sticks! The path from the bridge leads to another of Ynys Dawela's access points, which is handy for anyone walking to the nature park, although car parking at this entrance is extremely limited.

Back on the path, a sharp climb lies ahead! Follow the flight of steps – we counted 91 in all! Can you run up them all without stopping?

At the top of the steps is another three-way fork. Take the middle option, which initially goes straight ahead and then bends left to run parallel to the lower path we've just come along. The trail winds its way back towards the pond through a further meadow, and there is also the option of exploring another area of the park by following the Woodland Walk sign, which takes a short detour into the top of the park.

This grass-roofed shelter is an unexpected sight!

Back at the pond, there is still more to see before following the track uphill back to Llandeilo Road. Look across the disused car park and you'll spot a second, slightly more unusual shelter tucked away in a small woodland clearing. It blends into the surroundings perfectly, as its pillars look like tree trunks and it has a grass roof! It's a unique shelter for a picnic, with more great views.

The hardest part of the Secret Trail is deciding whether or not to tell anyone about it when you get home! To keep this secluded hideaway to yourself or to share the secret is up to you!

WALK 10
Reservoirs to Romans, Carmarthen

Carmarthen claims to be the oldest town in Wales and, whether this is true or not, its history makes for a brilliant day out with children. There is so much to see in a relatively small space, with myths, legends and some gruesome facts to discover along the trail! Merlin the Magician, who was a friend of King Arthur, is said to have been born in a cave outside the town and the name Carmarthen comes from the Welsh 'Caerfyrddin', which means Merlin's Fort. But whether he was born here or whether this was made up to make the town famous is up to you to decide!

The Romans arrived here more than 2,000 years ago and a considerable amount of their rich history can still be seen around the town. One of the most important buildings for the Romans was an impressive amphitheatre, in which could fit 5,000 spectators. After the Romans lost power, the amphitheatre was forgotten about for 1,500 years! It was discovered again about 40 years ago and is one of the highlights of the trail, making a brilliant natural playground for would-be gladiators. Another must-see attraction on the route is Carmarthen Castle, which has more within its ruined walls than first meets the eye.

Approx. distance	3.5 miles
Approx. time	2 hours+
Starting point	Cwmoernant Reservoirs, Tanerdy, Carmarthen
Grading	A town trail mainly along pavements and tarmac paths
Suggested age	5+
Map	OS Explorer178

The recommended starting point for the trail is Cwmoernant Reservoirs, two small reservoirs in the Tanerdy area about a mile from Carmarthen town centre. There are several car parks along this circular trail, giving families options about where to start and finish depending on what suits them best, but the reservoirs are in a peaceful, pretty spot that's ideal for a picnic at the end of a long walk. The reservoirs are also known as Cwmoernant Ponds and are now very popular for fishing.

From the reservoirs, follow Reservoir Road gently downhill to Priory Street, which is the main A484 through Carmarthen. Cross the road in front of the fuel station, taking care because it's a busy stretch with no dedicated crossing at this point. Look for the sign-posted public footpath that leads from Priory Street and follow the path through the trees. It circles a timber yard and becomes a wider, tarmac path running parallel to the A40 dual carriageway. This is also a cycle path, and blue signs show both the walking and cycling times to the town centre from here.

Cwmoernant Reservoirs are the start and finish point

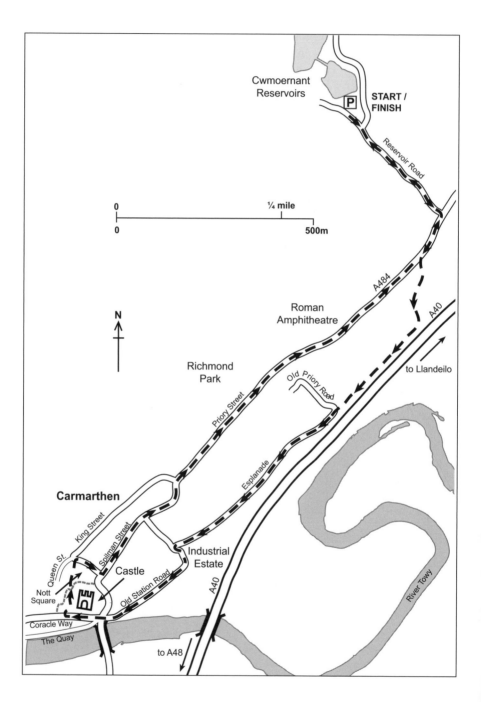

Cwmoernant
Reservoirs

START /
FINISH

P

Reservoir Road

0 ¼ mile
0 500m

N

A484

A40

Roman
Amphitheatre

to Llandeilo

Richmond
Park

Old Priory Road

Priory Street

Esplanade

Carmarthen

King Street

Spilman Street

Industrial
Estate

Castle

Old Station Road

A40

Queen St.

Nott
Square

River Towy

Coracle Way

The Quay

to A48

A short distance on, the path reaches the junction of Esplanade and Old Priory Road. The trail continues along Esplanade but, first, take a detour into Old Priory Road, where the priory once stood. It was here, 800 years ago, that a monk wrote the *Black Book of Carmarthen*, containing stories of Merlin and Arthur and said to be the oldest book written in Welsh to still survive today! There are no remains of the priory to see, but on the opposite side of the large field is something that young children will find far more exciting – a play area!

Back on Esplanade, walk past the cottages and through a wooden gate. The trail is stony here and cuts across a stretch of wasteland. It's not a pretty section of the walk but it's not far from here to the castle. At the far end of the wasteland is an industrial estate car park exiting onto Old Station Road. Follow this road left, past offices and an auction house, to the junction. To the left is the River Tywi and to the right is Castle Hill. You can walk up Castle Hill from here and cut in front of the big County Hall building to the castle, or walk straight ahead along Coracle Way, below the castle walls, and take the steps on the right hand side to the castle. Either way, it's a steep climb!

The castle is a ruin, but it's a highlight of the trail as within its walls is Castle House, a Victorian jail, where visitors can go into the cells and find out what it would have been like to be locked up in the olden days! Events days are held throughout the summer, where you can take part in a walking tour and listen to stories about the prisoners who were held here. Castle House is also where you'll find Carmarthen's tourist information centre, and we can vouch for the staff there being very friendly and keen to help!

The castle was built by King Henry I more than 900 years ago, and was one of the biggest and most important in Wales. Henry was one of the Normans, who were at war with Wales for centuries, and the Welsh prince Owain Glyndwr later captured the castle. Carmarthen Castle is also important for its links to Edmund Tudor. You might not have heard of him but his son, Henry, is more famous as he became Henry VII, the first Tudor king. Edmund died at Carmarthen Castle in 1456, before Henry was even born further west in Pembroke Castle.

The far-reaching views across the Tywi and Carmarthen's famous bridges are also another reason to visit the castle. Carmarthen used to be a busy port, and sail and steam ships would journey up the river to the town, bringing supplies of vinegar, sugar, fruit, ginger and marmalade. All of these things are easy to buy today but in those days were luxuries that most people couldn't afford. The Tywi is also home to a great deal of birds, butterflies and wild plants.

Facing the old police station inside the castle wall and the tourist information centre, go through the gate to your left into Nott Square. This used to be a busy market street and from here you can get to Carmarthen's many shops and cafés. With the castle behind you and the statue in front, turn right and walk across the pedestrianised square to Queen Street. Turn right into Queen Street then left onto Spilman Street, which also forms part of the A484 and marks the last leg of the trail back to the reservoirs.

Carmarthen Castle houses a Victorian jail and an information centre

Along Spilman Street look out on the left for Bank House, which was once where Carmarthenshire County Council was based. Today hundreds of people work for the council, relying on computers to do their job, but 100 years ago only 30 people worked at the council, sharing three typewriters and one phone!

The trail continues along Spilman Street, passing St Peter's Church, which is one of Carmarthen's oldest buildings. At the mini-roundabout, turn right and you're back in Priory Street. Continue along the road, passing Richmond Park School on the left. It's worth noting that next to the school is a public car park, which can be used as an alternative start and finish point for the walk if you prefer

The trail continues to the junction of Priory Street and Old Oak Lane, where an oak tree - known in Welsh as Yr Hen Dderwen and said to be more than 300 years old - used to stand. You can read more about it on the noticeboard before continuing along Priory Street to the amphitheatre. This was was built by the Romans and is thought to be one of only seven remaining amphitheatres in the UK. An amphitheatre is a round arena used for fighting contests between gladiators, as well as games, parades, religious holidays and public executions!

After the amphitheatre fell out of use it gradually got covered by the land and wasn't rediscovered until the end of World War II, when the land was redeveloped for new homes. A surveyor realised it might be an important site and finally the land was dug up more than 20 years later. The wall around the arena was uncovered, as well as evidence of seating on the banks, and today it's an interesting site with plenty of space for youngsters to run around and use their imaginations! This is the place to burn it off any surplus energy after a long walk, and we can testify to the slopes of the amphitheatre being the perfect spot for having a go at one of the National Trust's '50 things to do before you're 11¾' - rolling down a hill!

Rolling down the hill at Carmarthen amphitheatre!

From the amphitheatre, there's just a short stretch remaining along Priory St before the trail brings you back to Reservoir Road and the ponds. If you have time to spare, there is much more to see and do in the town, whilst Carmarthen County Museum at nearby Abergwili has on display Roman artefacts dug up around the town, as well as the last piece of Merlin's Oak!

WALK 11
The Lady of the Lake, Llyn y Fan Fach, Carmarthenshire

With Llyn y Fan Fach the only place in Wales named by Lonely Planet as one of the 1,000 must-see sights in the world, it easily forms one of Carmarthenshire's most iconic landscapes. In a remote spot, this enticing and mysterious lake is full of legend and is an ideal introduction to hill walking for children.

Approx. distance	2.5 miles (or an extended route of 6 miles)
Approx. time	2 hours (or 4-5 hours)
Starting point	Grid Reference SN 798238, Blaenau, Llanddeusant
Grading	A steep climb along a mountain track
Suggested age	6+
Map	OS Explorer OL12

Finding the starting point of this invigorating walk in the stunning Carmarthen Fans could be said to be the hard part! The tiny village of Llanddeusant, a few miles east of Llandeilo, is suggested in some guides as the starting point. Parking here, however, means an additional hike of almost two miles each way along an extremely narrow, winding country lane, making an already challenging trail for children a little too difficult.

A much better starting point is the small car park at the end of the waterboard track near Blaenau Farm (it's worth noting that there's a village called Blaenau further to the west of Carmarthenshire – don't get the two mixed up!). Drive through Llanddeusant and keep going along the lane until you pass the farm buildings. From Llanddeusant there are a number of small road signs pointing you in the right direction, as well as signs telling drivers where *not* to park!

The car park is on the right hand side between the road and the River Sawdde and there's also an information board about Llyn y Fan Fach and the Fforest Fawr Geopark. It's a beautiful spot and, after a long walk on a hot day, a paddle in the river is very tempting. But this is inadvisable for young children as the water can be fast flowing and very slippery underfoot. Note also that the car park is relatively small and it's a good idea to arrive early on warm days in the summer, when the route is likely to be popular.

From the car park you can see the peak of Picws Du in front of you, rising between two smaller hills. Picws Du, or the Black Peak, is the highest point in the Carmarthen Fans and forms part of the long ridge above Llyn y Fan Fach. Picws Du is too far for young children to walk whilst the lake, even though it can't be seen from this spot, is much

The distinctive peak of Picws Du overlooks this steep mountain climb

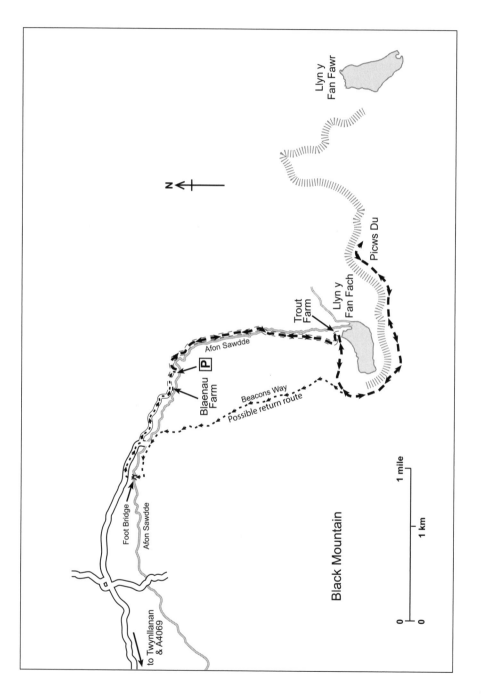

Llyn y Fan Fawr

Picws Du

Trout Farm

Llyn y Fan Fach

Afon Sawdde

P

Blaenau Farm

Beacons Way

Possible return route

Foot Bridge

Afon Sawdde

to Twynllanan & A4069

Black Mountain

N

0   1 km

0   1 mile

closer than the peak. Even so, reaching the lake involves a steady and relatively steep climb of more than a mile, so it's not really suitable for very young children or pushchairs.

Follow the track uphill in the direction of Picws Du, crossing a series of stone bridges over tributary streams along the way. After half a mile the track reaches a trout farm and bears through a wall to the left of the weir. Beyond the trout farm the track widens again and soon Llyn y Fan Fawr looms into view.

The trout farm on the Afon Sawdde on the way to Llyn y Fan Fach

Llyn y Fan Fach translates as 'the lake of the small hill'. A few miles to the east is Llyn y Fan Fawr, 'fawr' meaning big. It's possible for adults and older children to walk between the two peaks in a day and it's also possible to enjoy a walk to Llyn y Fan Fawr from the Swansea Valley – a surprisingly long drive from Llanddeusant given the lakes' proximity to each other.

The path continues ahead and loops round to the left, under the brow of a hillock, and suddenly the sparkling, clear blue lake is in front of you. In the late morning, the sun is ahead and high above the ridge, leaving the flank of the mountain looking dark and formidable, and it's easy to see why such mystery and legend surrounds Llyn y Fan Fach!

According to the legend, a farmer called Rhiwallon met a beautiful woman called Nelferch on the shores of Llyn y Fan Fach, where she was combing her golden hair in the reflection of the lake. She agreed to marry Rhiwallon but warned she would leave him if he gave her three causeless blows. They married and lived happily for years, bringing up three sons.

But, over the years and without meaning to each time, Rhiwallon gave Nelferch the three causeless blows he had promised not to. The first was by playfully flicking her with his glove to hurry her up on their way to a wedding. The second was by tapping her on the shoulder at a christening and the third was comforting her at a funeral. Nelferch said she must leave him forever and returned to the lake.

Rhiwallon was heartbroken and died soon afterwards. But their three sons were allowed to visit their mother at the lake, where she told them to become healers and showed them where to find healing herbs. They became known as the Physicians of Myddfai, and their children and grandchildren are said to have continued the tradition for hundreds of years!

There is no defined path around the lake and to walk around it would involve scrambling over rocks, stony ground and mountain streams, so it's advisable to stay on the same shore as the dam. Even on the sunniest day, there can be a sharp breeze by the lake, so have gloves and hats in your rucksack just in case.

Children aged up to six or seven will probably have walked far enough by this point. Energetic older children, however, might want to follow the well-defined path leading from the right of the dam to the ridge. It's a steep climb but the views of Llyn y Fan Fach from the ridge are well worth the effort. The ridge circles around the lake, stretching ahead to Picws Du. From here, the walk to the cairn marking Picws Du is relatively flat and extends the distance to a six-mile round trail. Beyond Picws Du are Fan Foel and the long ridge of Fan Hir, which runs above Llyn y Fan Fawr – but this is a *long* hike!

Even if you decide not to continue to Picws Du, it's worth making the climb a little way along the ridge for the stunning panoramic views. To the south west, on a clear day, the Carmarthenshire coast is visible, whilst to the north you can see Usk Reservoir and across the Brecon Beacons National Park.

The recommended return trail follows the way you came, heading back down the ridge to the dam and back onto the track. It's possible, as you round the bowl above the lake and before the steep descent off the ridge, to continue straight ahead onto a grassy footpath. This forms part of the Brecon Way and runs over the hillock and back down to the River Sawdde. But unfortunately, although it brings you nearly directly opposite the car park, there's no crossing place over the

Llyn y Fan Fach from Picws Du

Sawdde at this point! The footpath continues away from Blaenau Farm for about a mile, where it's then possible to cross the river and walk back up the track to the starting point. It's a pleasant alternative but, again, isn't easy for small children and depends on energy levels, so think carefully before you commit to it or or instead stick to the gravel track along which we walked up to the lake earlier.

WALK 12
Walk the Worm, Rhossili, Gower

If you haven't already visited Rhossili on the south western tip of the Gower peninsula, it's a must to put at the top of your travel wish list. Rhossili Bay is consistently voted amongst the best beaches not just in the UK but in the world and, looking across its three miles of golden sand and dramatic, jagged coastline, it's easy to understand why.

Approx. distance	5 miles
Approx. time	3 hours
Starting point	National Trust visitor centre and shop, Rhossili, Gower
Grading	A very challenging walk with several sections of scrambling
Suggested age	8+
Map	OS Explorer 164

Synonymous with Rhossili is Worms Head, a one-mile-long slither of rock stretching into the sea that is, for most of the time, cut off from the mainland. It was given its name by Viking invaders who thought it looked like a sea serpent or dragon, the Norse word for which is 'wurm'. It's accessible via a tidal causeway for only two and a half hours before and after low tide every day, which, for many walkers, only adds to the attraction and sense of adventure.

But with adventure comes risk, and this really is the most challenging trail in the book. It's essential that families undertaking the walk to the Worm do not underestimate the effort involved or the risk in

Worms Head from Rhossili cliffs

trying to swim or paddle back to the mainland if caught out by the returning tide. However calm the water looks and however near the shore seems, the currents are treacherous. That said, with careful planning and a lot of common sense, this is an exhilarating trail, giving older children who can keep a good pace a real sense of achievement and some spectacular memories to take home.

Eight is advised as the minimum age for this walk, although energetic six year olds have done it whilst some children older than eight will feel unconfident on the rocks. It's also important that parents are fit and have a good head for heights! I would advise against carrying babies and toddlers in slings and back carriers, due to the potential for slipping on the rocks, but again it's for each family to consider depending on their own fitness and experience. Walking boots are also advised, rather than sandals or trainers.

It's also advisable to plan this walk in advance, rather than turning up on a sunny day and hoping the tide times match your schedule! Tide

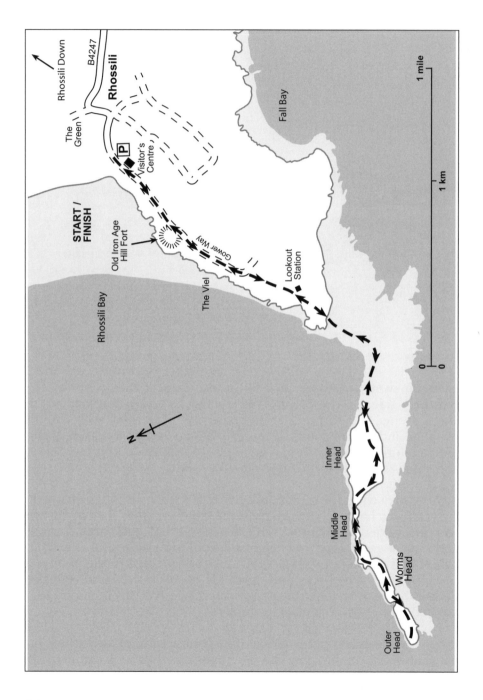

Rhossili Down

B4247

Rhossili

The Green

P

Visitor's Centre

START / FINISH

Old Iron Age Hill Fort

Rhossili Bay

The Viel

Gower Way

Lookout Station

Fall Bay

Inner Head

Middle Head

Worms Head

Outer Head

N

1 mile

1 km

0

0

tables are available from the National Trust visitor centre and shop, which is the starting point for the walk, as well as at the coastguard hut immediately before the tidal causeway crossing and online. It's also worth noting that Outer Head is closed to visitors between 1st March and 15th August every year due to nesting birds. This leaves little more than half the year in which visitors can walk the full length of the Worm, although the journey across Inner and Middle Head alone is certainly worth making.

The Gower peninsula was, in 1956, the first place in the UK to be named an Area of Outstanding Natural Beauty. Much of Gower, including Worms Head, is now owned and protected by the National Trust, and Trust staff and volunteers are active all year round in maintaining its natural beauty and improving accessibility. There is a car park behind the visitor centre, which is not owned by the National Trust and cost £3 to park in at the time of publication. Alternatively, walkers are able to use the car park at St Mary's Church, half a mile further back in Rhossili village, which is cheaper and has an honesty box. There is a toilet block next to the visitor centre.

If your children are too young for the Worm or you feel it's too adventurous, there is still plenty of land for families to explore along Rhossili's fabulous coastline. The first section of the walk – from the visitor centre to the coastguard hut – is worth making for the views of the Worm and across Rhossili Bay. The National Trust also has lovely tracker packs with bug catchers, binoculars, activity sheets and nature cards, and staff have also created family-friendly geocaching trails, which can be followed with GPS devices hired from the visitor centre for a fully returnable £5 deposit. The toddler trail takes children on a

The National Trust has fun tracker packs for children's trails

hunt for several letters on wooden posts along a short stretch of the coastal path, which they have to use at the end to make a seaside word. Another geocaching trail across Rhossili Down is longer and more suitable for older children, as it can take a couple of hours.

From the visitor centre, turn left and follow the cliff-top path in the direction of the Worm. The distinctive flat top of Inner Head looks gentle and hospitable from this distance! As the path widens, look for the ridges and dips of an Iron Age hill fort on the right, between the path and the sea. It's known as Old Castle Camp and promontory forts like this were placed on cliff tops with good views all around to see the enemy coming.

The trail then passes the Viel, which is a medieval open field strip system of farming between Rhossili village and the sea, and the Fairway. The Fairway approaches the coastguard hut, which has further reminders of tide times on a sign in the window. Don't be surprised if the coastguard pops out and asks if you're crossing, as they are here to keep track of walkers! Although it can be hard to peel your eyes off the Worm, take time to look north and to the ridge of Rhossili Down above the beach. At more than 600 feet, it's the highest point on the peninsula and evidence of life on Gower thousands of years ago has been found on the top.

In front of the coastguard hut, a flight of wide steps, created and maintained by Trust volunteers, leads down to the causeway *(the author has a vested interest here as her mum and dad are dedicated volunteers!)*. There is an unmissable 'danger' sign at the head of the rocks, which should be read no matter how well you've planned, then it's time to start picking out a route across the causeway. A good tip is to keep to the right as much as possible because, when the tide is far out, a narrow 'beach' of sorts is formed and is a little flatter than the rocks to walk across.

The causeway is approximately half a mile long but can take about half an hour to walk across due to its rugged nature and the care required. At the foot of the Worm, take a look at the hefty bell attached to the 'danger' sign. It's here in case you do become cut off, and it's far better to use it to raise the alarm than risk the incoming tide. Hopefully it won't be needed – but it's reassuring to know it's here!

Determined legwork is needed to reach this point, but the scrambling isn't over yet. From some angles on the mainland it can be hard to see that the Worm is actually split into three sections, Inner, Middle and Outer Head. Inner Head is the biggest and offers two options;

Crossing the tidal causeway towards Inner Head

following the narrow but clear path running along the foot or – yes, of course! – climbing up and following the ridge. It looks formidable but, although steep, it's only a short climb and the views are worth it. Whichever way you choose, take care as the grass can be springy and there are plenty of hidden rabbit holes that can cause a nasty turned ankle.

Autumn is the time of year when grey seals give birth and Inner Head offers a bird's eye view of the mother seals and their calves on the rocks below. Just take care to peer over carefully and quietly, to avoid startling them. At the far end of the ridge, Outer Head comes into view. It's even more enticing closer up and easily shows why Rhossili Bay rivals some of the best beaches in the world.

The rocky section to Middle Head is called Low Neck, and crossing it takes a bit more energy-zapping scrambling. It appears as though the quickest option is to plough straight ahead over the rocks to the ridge, but this is harder than it seems and it's easier to venture down onto the flat, rocky plateau and cover a bit of ground before heading upwards to the right again. There is no defined path to reach the ridge and all routes involve a climb at some point, but a good marker to aim for is the slightly larger slabs below the landmark natural archway. This is Devil's Bridge, made of limestone and all that remains of a collapsed sea cave. It's thought that the bridge will eventually collapse one day too.

Middle Head, with Devil's Bridge, and Outer Head

One the other side of Devil's Bridge, the path continues to the left and towards Outer Head. This is the point at which walkers must stop during the nesting season, with a sign clearly stating that birds such as guillemots, razorbills, peregrines and gulls must not be disturbed. If you are able to continue, however, it's a short climb from here to the very top of Outer Head, a towering slab of rock standing majestically on what seems to be the edge of the world when you're on it! It can be blustery and good balance is needed but it's an incredibly rewarding climb. Take a look into the blow hole, where the air being pushed up from the waves below has been described as 'nature's hairdryer'!

Take extra care walking back, as children might be tiring by now and careless slips and falls can happen. At the far end of Inner Head, look carefully at the tide and make sure you have enough time to get across safely. The poet and writer Dylan Thomas, who you can read more about in Chapter Six, claimed to have been trapped for several hours after falling asleep on Inner Head, with little more than some sandwiches and a good book to keep him company!

Back on the mainland, Rhossili Beach is the perfect place for a rest after a long, demanding walk. There are often surfers and hang-gliders to watch and another interesting sight, when the tide is out, is the wreck of a ship called *Helvetia*. It was blown onto the beach during a storm in 1887 and the remains of its wooden frame can be seen sticking out of the sand. Its bow is higher than the rest of the ship and some people think that, from a certain angle, it resembles the Worms Head!

WALK 13
The Swansea Bay Way, Swansea

If you don't know Swansea very well, don't make the mistake of thinking it's Cardiff's poor relation. The 'ugly lovely town' has undergone something of a revival in recent years, rebranding itself as Wales' waterfront city and smartening up its act. The result is an inviting, diverse tourist hotspot, small enough to retain its friendliness yet with more than enough to rival the vibrancy of the capital along the M4.

Approx. distance	5.5 miles
Approx. time	3 hours
Starting point	The National Waterfront Museum, Swansea Marina
Grading	A level, linear seaside walk along tarmac
Suggested age	All ages; pushchair friendly
Map	OS Explorer 165

Swansea Bay is a five-mile stretch circling from the Maritime Quarter to Mumbles, an ever-popular seaside town declared, by my children following extensive research, to sell the best ice cream in the world. This trail is a linear walk around the bay that we've graded suitable for all ages because of its accessibility, but note that it is a long way and walking the whole length might prove too much for younger children.

Instead, though, the route can be walked in sections or you can even walk some of it before hopping on one of the regular buses that travel alongside the trail and reaching Mumbles with a little help! As it's a linear route, the bus service is also the way to return to the Maritime Quarter from Mumbles at the end of the trail.

The walk starts at the National Waterfront Museum, a beautiful red brick and glass building between the LC2 Leisure Complex and the marina. There is a large car park in front of the LC2, off Oystermouth Road (the A4067), which costs £5 for a stay of more than four hours, a necessary timescale for this walk by the time you factor in the return bus journey.

To start the trail, walk through or around the museum to the waterfront, where a tugboat and a lightship are permanently docked. More can be read about them and their history on the information board. Follow the marina to the right along Victoria Quay, dipping in and out of the cover of arcades of shops and cafés. At the end of the marina, follow the path left towards the towering building on the opposite side of the water, called, appropriately, The Tower. It's the tallest building in Wales and consists mainly of apartments, but at the top is a restaurant – with amazing views, obviously!

Cross the road in front of The Tower, carefully, as it's on a corner, and take the zig-zag steps ahead to the seafront. A sharp breeze might

There is a lot to see at Swansea Marina

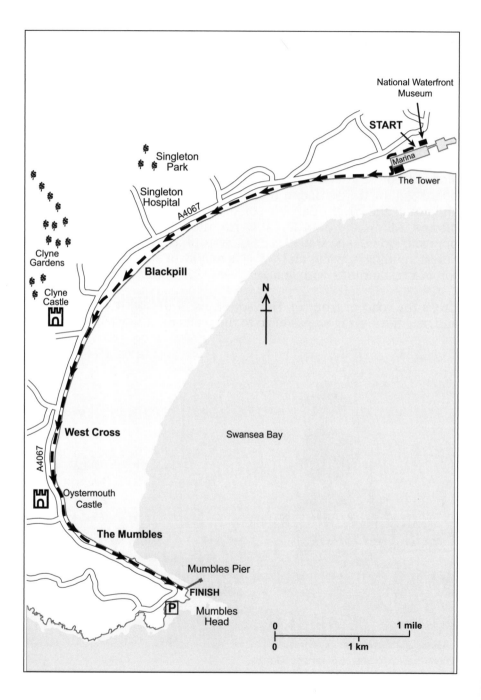

National Waterfront Museum

START

Marina

The Tower

Singleton Park

Singleton Hospital

A4067

Clyne Gardens

Clyne Castle

Blackpill

N

West Cross

A4067

Oystermouth Castle

The Mumbles

Swansea Bay

Mumbles Pier

FINISH

P

Mumbles Head

| 0 | | 1 mile |
| 0 | 1 km | |

meet you at the top! Swansea Bay opens out in front of the promenade, with views on a clear day to the hills above Port Talbot to the east and Mumbles, with its distinctive head, to the west.

Follow the promenade towards Mumbles, passing the concrete steps down to the beach. The building on the right is Swansea's civic centre, and this marks the start of the Swansea Prom Fitness Trail, a 2.5m route between here and Blackpill. Designed to encourage people to enjoy the fresh air and get fit in a fun environment, the trail has outdoor gym equipment for everyone to use and is also popular with walkers, joggers, cyclists and skaters.

The path becomes sandier as it approaches a children's play area on the beach, designed quite literally in ship-shape and with slides, a lookout and climbing walls. At this point the trail joins the pavement alongside the busy Oystermouth Road. It's a noisy stretch and the least pleasant section of the trail, but it's not for long.

Pass the signs pointing right to Swansea Guildhall and the Brangwyn Hall, an attractive civic building used for concerts and events. From several points along this trail the Guildhall's clock tower is visible above the rooftops. Also on the opposite side of the road is St Helen's Rugby and Cricket Ground and the Patti Pavilion.

The Pavilion was named after world-famous opera singer Dame Adelina Patti, who owned Craig y Nos Castle in the Swansea Valley and built the Patti Pavilion as her winter gardens before donating it to the city. At one point it became so run down it was known locally as the 'tatty Patti', but a refurbishment has transformed it back into an elegant concert hall and restaurant.

Just past the Patti, on the trail side of the road, is a café bar, water sports centre and public toilets. From here the path rises away from the road and becomes more enjoyable again. Walkers and cyclists share the trail, with a continual white line along the middle to divide the two, so take care to stick to the right side!

The trail runs through a pleasant avenue towards a memorial built to honour the men who died in the South African War more than 100 years ago. Soon after this war came World War I, and a larger memorial to the soldiers of this and World War II is a short distance along the path. 2014 marks 100 years since the start of World War I, so it's a good chance to find out more. Look for the stone laid by Earl Haig, one of the most senior officers of the war, who placed a King's shilling under the plaque. A shilling was a coin that was commonly used before 'new' money was introduced in the 1970s. It roughly equates to 5p today, although a shilling then could buy more than 5p does now!

As the path passes Swansea University on the opposite side of Oystermouth Road, several items of outdoor gym equipment are lined up as part of the Prom Trail. Have a go! Just past the university is Singleton Park, which is an ideal place to stop if the entire walk to Mumbles is too far. Within Singleton Park is a boating lake, crazy golf and the beautiful Botanical Gardens, set within an old walled garden. There are also regular buses back to Swansea from here.

If you plan to continue to Mumbles, there are some distractions coming up! Near the three-mile mark is a pitch and putt green and a skate park, as well as the start of the Swansea Bay Rider land train route. The train runs between Blackpill and Mumbles, although it's not guaranteed if the weather is poor. A short distance beyond the pitch and putt green, the path veers left over a small wooden bridge and brings you to Blackpill Lido. This is a lovely place to cool down on a hot day and has a café, public toilets and an ice cream kiosk.

Blackpill Lido proves the perfect pit stop!

From the lido, the trail stays close to the sea, with great views as it gets closer and closer towards Mumbles. If you look back at this point, you might be surprised at how far you've walked! On the opposite side of the road, a short way past the lido, is Clyne Gardens, another of Swansea's jewels. Every May, when certain species such as rhododendrons are looking their best, the gardens marks 'Clyne in Bloom', whilst other highlights include the bluebell wood, a Japanese bridge, several family trails and a delightful, carved 'story tree'.

By the time the trail reaches Mumbles, you've clocked up five miles – and there's still another half mile to go if you want to reach the Victorian pier! Alternatively, leave the promenade and join Mumbles Road until reaching the mini roundabout outside the White Rose pub on the corner. Turn right into Newton Road and then right again into Castle Avenue where, ahead, is Oystermouth Castle.

Much conservation work has taken place at the castle in recent years. Previously closed sections are now open to the public and a glass bridge has been installed in the chapel. Admission charges are low and provide excellent value for money, with lots of historical secrets waiting to be discovered! The grounds around the castle are also attractive and offer a welcome and peaceful place for a rest and have a snack after the long trail.

If you want to walk further still, continue along the promenade, in the shadow of Knab Rock, to Mumbles Pier, which has a very eventful history! Opened at the end of the 19th century it was originally an

Mumbles Pier has been extensively refurbished

'overflow' drop-off for cargo heading to Swansea Docks, but soon tourists were arriving there on steamboats. In the 1920s the landmark red-roofed building was added but, during World War II, it was used by the army and not very carefully looked after.

In the 1950s the pier was given a major revamp but, for the next 60 years, little work was carried out. It was closed to the public in 2011 and has since undergone a major restoration, with a new lifeboat station being built at the end of the pier and a new visitor complex created. In 2014 it opened to a limited number of visitors and the plan is for it to re-open fully in the future.

Even with the pier closed, the walk to it is worth making for the views back across the bay to Swansea – not to mention Verdi's, a large, glass-fronted ice cream parlour overlooking the sea. The renowned Joe's Ice Cream is also based in Mumbles, leaving walkers spoilt for choice!

To return to Swansea, walk back to the White Rose and look for the bus stop a short distance past the mini-roundabout, in the direction of Swansea. Regular buses return to the city centre, diverging from Oystermouth Road at the rugby and cricket ground and following St Helen's Road past the Guildhall and to the Quadrant bus station.

The National Waterfront Museum is just a few minutes' walk from here. Leave the bus station by walking right, to the end of the line of bus bays, and exiting through the door facing Tesco. Follow the pavement around the supermarket car park back to Oystermouth Road, taking care when crossing to the LC2 as it's a busy road with multiple lanes. A set of traffic lights and a crossing is a little further along the road. Walk around the leisure centre and back to the museum starting point.

The museum, built in a converted Edwardian dockside warehouse that was used more recently as Swansea's Industrial and Maritime Museum, was opened in 2005 and has proved one of our favourite attractions ever since. Children love its unfussy, hands-on attitude and tons of space, whilst it's a winner for parents due to its free admission, in line with all national museums in Wales, although donations are welcomed.

The museum is strong on Swansea's industrial past and there's a particular focus on transport, which keeps engine-obsessed children fully engaged! In the transport hall at the front of the museum, make sure to look up or you'll miss the magnificent flying machine! There's also a very important life-sized model to look out for at the end of this hall. Did you know that the very first railway steam journey happened in Wales? It took place more than 200 years ago in Merthyr Tydfil with a locomotive engine built by a man called Richard Trevithick. A replica of the tram is on display here and on certain days staff fire her up and drive her along the track outside!

There's more to see in the museum grounds, including the UK's only surviving canal boat weighing bridge. This was used to weigh barges and their cargoes on the Glamorganshire so the correct toll could be worked out. The museum also houses the Waterfront Café, which has refreshingly healthy choices on the menu and which has held a number of centenary events celebrating the life of poet and playwright Dylan Thomas.

The Dylan Thomas Centenary Walk in Chapter Six gives much more information about Dylan. Laugharne was the place he loved and spent the last years of his life in, but he was born and grew up in Swansea and the city holds many events commemorating the poet and his work, including an annual festival in October. The Dylan Thomas Centre, also in the Maritime Quarter, is a short walk from the National Waterfront Museum.

WALK 14
The River Trail, Clydach, Swansea

Clydach is a large village in the Swansea Valley with lots of green space on the doorstep, including woodland, parks, hills and a stretch of the Swansea Canal. This short trail runs from the popular Forge Fach Park in the heart of Clydach to the Cwm Clydach RSPB Reserve, a small and peaceful wildlife haven on the edge of the countryside.

Approx. distance	2 miles
Approx. time	1 hour
Starting point	Forge Fach Park, Hebron Road, Clydach
Grading	An easy walk along mainly level paths
Suggested age	All ages; pushchair friendly
Map	OS Explorer 165

This trail is a trip down memory lane for me, having grown up in Clydach and having spent much of my childhood playing on the banks of the Lower Clydach River and in Forge Fach Park. The park has changed a lot since those days, when, if children weren't playing unsupervised along the riverbank, we were in the outdoor swimming baths at Forge Fach Park. Clydach Baths was built in 1925, when it was rare for a public pool to be owned by the parish council. The baths figure strongly in the memories of many local people living in Clydach before the 1990s but, sadly for nostalgia, they have since been demolished.

Forge Fach Park has been regenerated in the last 10 years, with a new community centre, café, day nursery and children's adventure play

There is a lot to see on this trail!

park. At the time of writing, the future of the centre and park was in doubt following financial difficulties within the Cwmni Clydach Development Trust, with Swansea Council taking control in the interim. The trail itself, however, remains accessible at all times, as it starts from a footpath running outside the park railings, between the park and the river.

Forge Fach Park is on the corner of Hebron Road and the High Street, an area known as 'the Square' and which is at the heart of 'old' Clydach. Clydach used to be a tiny village but the creation of the Swansea Canal brought more people to live and trade here. It was the coming of a nickel works at the other end of the High Street, however, that really put Clydach on the map and caused the population to boom. The Mond works, founded by a German man called Ludwig Mond, opened in 1902 and, at one time, four out of every ten people living in Clydach worked there. The works is still running today, although fewer people work there now.

From Hebron Road, follow the narrow riverside path to the right of Forge Fach Park. The Lower Clydach River runs through Cwm Clydach and meets the larger River Tawe just a short distance south of Forge Fach. The path quickly draws level with the top of the park, where steps to the right lead to the riverbank and views of Forge Fach Waterfall, which used to power a mill. From the top of the steps, continue straight ahead, with the river on your right and the remains of a canal bed on the left. Cross the tiny stone bridge over the canal bed and walk up the flight of steps, turning right at the top onto a wider path.

A short distance along is an idyllic riverbank spot for a picnic and safe wading. Continuing along the path to the fork, stay left on the main track, where you'll soon pass a bridge on the right, with an aged turnstile in front of it. Across this bridge are Forge Cottages, a very old row of houses originally built for forge workers. The path can get

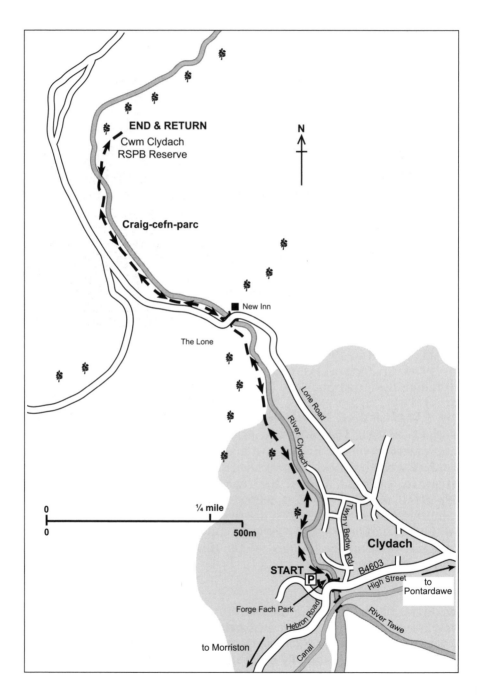

END & RETURN
Cwm Clydach
RSPB Reserve

Craig-cefn-parc

N

■ New Inn

The Lone

0
¼ mile
0
500m

Lone Road

River Clydach

Twyn y Bedw Rd

Clydach

B4603

START
P

High Street
to
Pontardawe

Forge Fach Park

Hebron Road

River Tawe

to Morriston

Canal

The River Trail follows a pretty woodland path

quite muddy along this stretch, so wellies are a good idea generally, and not just for wearing to paddle in the river!

Pass the bridge leading to Forge Cottages. The countryside now opens up and the trail runs alongside a wide field with clear views of the mountain ahead. The horses in the field are very friendly and seem to enjoy attention! Continue past the second paddock, the stables and a row of cottages. This lane is called The Lone and it meets Lone Road, the main route between Clydach and the next village of Craig Cefn Parc. Look right, where, over the bridge, you might see a number of very old campervans waiting to be restored in the workshop next to the New Inn.

Take care crossing the road as this spot is on a sharp double bend and there is no pavement. The path ahead now enters the steep-sided Cwm Clydach RSBP Reserve, which was created in 1987 after the RSBP bird organisation discovered many breeding birds here. The site is now a haven for buzzards, red kites, green and great spotted woodpeckers, treecreepers, dippers and bullfinches, as well as small birds such as willow warblers and pied flycatchers. They travel all the way from South Africa to spend their summers here and the RSPB provides and maintains nesting boxes for them.

The reserve is also home to otters and many species of insect and butterfly, including less common breeds such as the beautiful silver-washed fritillary. In summer many colourful flowers grow here but perhaps the best time to see the reserve is in the spring, when the bluebells and the wood anemones are in bloom.

Until 1962 this area was a working coalmining valley, with more than 1,000 workers employed at Cwm Clydach. The biggest colliery opened in 1863 and was known locally as Nixon's. There are plenty of signs of the former mines throughout the reserve and the valley, including the remains of buildings along the old tramway.

You can extend your walk from Forge Fach by completing one of the two trails around the reserve. The Nixon Trail, named after the coalmine, is an easy 1.5-mile circular route from the car park. The path is relatively flat and well maintained. The second trail is called the Trussler Trail and it starts along the same route as the Nixon but goes further, towards the east of the river. It includes some steep sections and can get very muddy in parts.

For adults and older children, the reserve is also the start of a nine-mile circular walk along the Lower Clydach River. It passes the 300-year-old Gellionen Chapel, which is known locally as the White Chapel and is said to be haunted! There are also some interesting archaeological

The Cwm Clydach RSPB Reserve is the habitat of the red kite
(*Photo by Ben Hall, rspb-images.com*)

sites, such as Carn Llechart, one of the biggest ring cairns in Wales, and spectacular views of the Brecon Beacons. A leaflet outlining the Cwm Clydach Walk can be downloaded at **www.swansea.gov.uk**

The Cwm Clydach RSPB Reserve and nature trails are open at all times and are free, but there is no lighting and some sections can be slippery. Dogs are welcome but must be kept on leads and walkers are asked to stay on the paths, as some of the ruined buildings and mines might be dangerous.

The trail returns along the same route to Forge Fach Park, where the wooden-frame adventure play park is ideal for younger children although, unfortunately, there have been complaints locally that the park is not always open at peak times. If you are able to enter the park, look out for the commemorative horse trough, which is very old and used to stand in the Square. It was built in memory of a man called William Henry Lewis and, when it was unveiled in 1907, a huge crowd turned up to watch!

There are several lovely walking routes from Clydach. Close to the River Trail is the Swansea Canal towpath, running from the village to the small town of Pontardawe further along the Swansea Valley. The canal towpath can be accessed on the other side of the Square, behind the old brick building that used to be Clydach Public Hall and is now the popular Dynamic Rock indoor climbing centre.

A mile or so along the towpath, before the village of Trebanos, is Clydach's largest park, Coed Gwilym. You can also reach it in the car by driving from Forge Fach Park along the High Street and Pontardawe Road. At Coed Gwilym is Clydach Heritage Centre, the place to find out more about Clydach's history, which runs interesting exhibitions and family events during weekends and school holidays. Coed Gwilym also has a large children's play area, fitness trail and canoe hire, whilst cyclists might want to know that the towpath forms part of Sustran's National Cycle Network Route 43.

WALK 15
Waterfall Walk, Pontneddfechan, Neath

On a clear, sunny day, Waterfall Country in the Vale of Neath is arguably one of the most beautiful spots in Wales. Deep in the Fforest Fawr Geopark, it's a series of dramatic gorges, rivers and waterfalls, with a rich history and stunning scenery. Many of the routes in Waterfall Country are perhaps a little too far and too challenging for young children, but the relatively gentle and short trail to Sgwd Gwladus is an excellent chance for families to get up close to one of nature's most spectacular sights.

Approx. distance	2.5 miles
Approx. time	1.5 hours
Starting point	Waterfalls Centre, Pontneddfechan, Neath
Grading	A woodland walk with a slight gradient and some slippery sections
Suggested age	4+
Map	OS ExplorerOL12

Unfortunately, its beauty and accessibility is no secret, and this trail from the small village of Pontneddfechan is a popular route, even early in the day. The car park can fill up by 9:30am and, once at Sgwd Gwladus, you might have to wait your turn to take photos unless you don't mind strangers in the background of your snaps! But the tranquillity enjoyed on some of the other trails in this book is a worthwhile sacrifice here, the steady stream of walkers and tourists worth putting up with for the remarkable views.

Waterfall Country is in the heart of the Vale of Neath

The walk starts from the Angel Inn in Pontneddfechan, which is on the main road opposite the Waterfalls Centre. A car park is next to the pub and there's also a small block of public toilets on the corner. The Waterfalls Centre is packed with information on the geopark, as well as many South Wales attractions, although we found online details about opening times – as well as the distance to the falls – to be misleading, so it's worth checking ahead of a visit. It's also worth noting there are no free waterfall trails maps available at the centre, the official area guide being £3.50, and that the geo activity backpacks are £5 to hire, *plus* a £10 returnable deposit, which, at the time of our visit, could only be paid in cash.

That said, the backpacks are excellent and certainly got the children in our group into the exploring spirit! The rucksacks come in black or pink and contain binoculars, bug catchers and lots of information about the wildlife you might see along the trail. There's also an activity booklet encouraging children to turn 'map detectives' and learn how to read basic grid references, as well as a survival challenge and

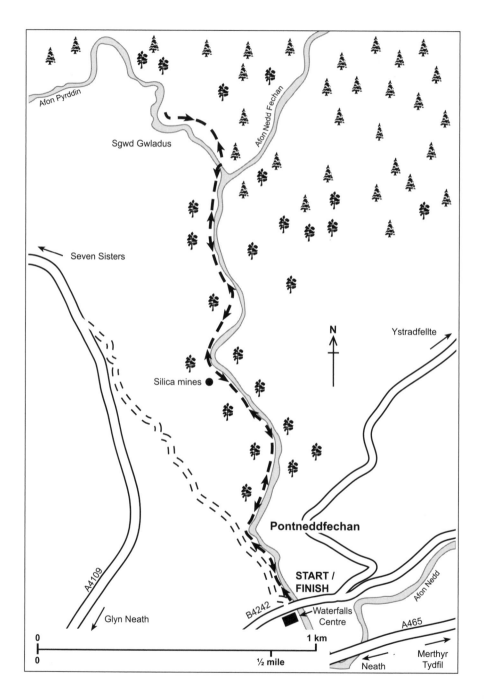

Afon Pyrddin

Sgwd Gwladus

Afon Nedd Fechan

Seven Sisters

N

Ystradfellte

Silica mines

Pontneddfechan

START /
FINISH

A4109

Glyn Neath

B4242

Waterfalls
Centre

Afon Nedd

A465

Merthyr
Tydfil

Neath

0
0

1 km

½ mile

minibeast Olympics. The pack undoubtedly increases excitement and engagement amongst children but, at £5 each and yet with nothing to take home other than the activity booklet, one between the group seemed like a good idea to us!

The geo activity backpacks contain lots to do!

Facing the Angel, follow the lane along the right hand side of the pub to the gateway signposted Waterfall Country. The trail runs alongside the river and for the first three quarters of a mile is fairly level. Some online routes mark the trail as being pushchair friendly but I'd have reservations about this, particularly the last section, which is very uneven and can be hazardous in poor weather.

There are many places along the way to climb down to the riverbank to watch the wildlife and, on our walk, some of our group were lucky enough to see a kingfisher swooping past in a flash of orange and turquoise. Shortly along the path you reach the ruins of an old corn mill, marked on the activity booklet map. A little further along are two entrances to silica mines, where silica rock, used to make quartz, was dug. Due to a certain popular computer game involving mines, these entrances sparked many questions on our walk about what used to happen underground!

Three quarters of a mile from the start, a short flight of wooden steps marks the beginning of a gentle climb to the falls. Soon after this, the trail reaches the meeting point of two rivers, the Nedd Fechan and the Afon Pyrddin. Cross the long wooden bridge and follow the Sgwd Gwladus sign left. Signposted in the opposite direction is a longer walk to Pont Melin-fach, which takes about half an hour from here and passes three further waterfalls, which, with Sgwd Gwladus, make the Four Falls Trail.

Continue left for a couple of minutes until Sgwd Gwladus appears. Also known as Lady Falls, the waterfall is named after a beautiful young woman reputed to be one of 24 daughters of a Welsh prince called Brychan of Brycheiniog. Gwladus fell in love with a man called Einion, but her love was not returned and she became destined to spend eternity flowing elegantly in the form of the waterfall. Einion was also immortalised in another waterfall, Sgwd Einion Gam, which is the highest falls in the Ystrafellte area and one of the most difficult to reach, with no footpath and five rivers to cross to get to it!

Sgwd Gwladus is in the Fforest Fawr Geopark

Sgwd Gwladus is one of the smaller falls and therefore the pool into which it tumbles is calm. It's a beautiful spot, with plenty of rocks to picnic on and a shingle 'beach' ideal for skimming stones. It's possible to walk behind the waterfall and also to its head on the rocky platform above. Wet rocks, of course, can be very slippery, so it might be advisable to try this only with older children.

Return to the Angel along the same path, now following the flow of the river. The Angel Inn is a pleasant and very popular place for meals, teas and coffees, whilst the Waterfalls Centre sells the distinctive Joe's ice cream, made in Swansea and renowned much further afield! You might also want to consider the Powder Trail, a short trail along an old tram road to a former gunpowder works and the watermills that powered it.

WALK 16
Cascade Escapade, Gnoll Estate Country Park, Neath

The Gnoll Estate Country Park is a surprisingly spacious park above the town of Neath, with more to do and see than first meets the eye. Admission to the estate itself is free and there's simply a £1 charge at the car park, giving fantastic value to families looking for an active day out in beautiful countryside. Because the Gnoll was built on the hillside, the views over Neath and the Vale of Neath are outstanding, so it's no surprise the estate has been voted Wales' best picnic spot in the National Picnic Awards!

Approx. distance	2 miles
Approx. time	1 hour
Starting point	Gnoll Estate Country Park visitor centre
Grading	A mainly level country park and woodland trail
Suggested age	4+
Map	OS Explorer 165

The Gnoll Estate Country Park also features in Chapter 17, which follows the path taken to work by a 19th century tinplate worker called Lucy Lewis. As explained in Chapter 17, the Lucy Lewis trail starts from the rear entrance to the Gnoll, which is accessed from the village of Tonna and along a different road. This trail, on the other hand, starts from the Gnoll's main visitor car park at the 'front' of the estate, which is accessed from Neath town centre and clearly marked by brown signs.

The Gnoll was the home of a rich family called the Mackworths, who lived in Gnoll House in the grounds. Sadly this mansion was demolished in 1957 but the foundations and cellars remain visible, whilst some of the other buildings and follies within the estate still stand and make quirky landmarks for children to find and explore.

The trail starts at the visitor centre, which is stocked full of information, has a café and toilets and is also the point where mobility scooters can be hired. From the visitor centre, follow the path past the children's play area, with the large lake on your left hand side. This is the Fishpond, which was created at the beginning of the 1700s when the Mackworth family was busy transforming the park. For the pond to be formed, a small road had to be flooded, which caused a fuss at the time! The Fishpond holds more than six million gallons of water and is the largest of several lakes at the Gnoll. Bird feed for the ducks and geese can be bought from the visitor centre and, if you plan your visit during the evening, bats can sometimes be seen flying over the lake.

At the far end of the lake, the path forks left and right. To the right is the site of Gnoll House, which includes an ice house and a grassy terrace, as well as a bamboo 'forest', which is great fun for children to play in! But the trail follows the left-hand fork across the bridge at the end of the Fishpond, passing the pretty Fishpond House. This was once lived in by the estate's bailiff, who was in charge of protecting the stock of carp in the water. From the bridge are views across the lake to the cascades.

Follow the path along the opposite bank of the lake in the shade of the trees until reaching a small wooden bridge, where the trail turns uphill alongside the cascades. It doesn't matter which side you walk along, as there are stepping stones halfway up and you can also cross at the top. These are the French Cascades, a recreation of the formal cascades made in the 1720s. When the estate fell into disuse, this attractive feature became covered by undergrowth and lay undiscovered until 1985, when renovations began and it was recreated.

The French Cascades are one of two sets of falls within the estate, the other being the informal cascades much further away from Gnoll House, at the top of Mosshouse Wood. The informal cascades have an

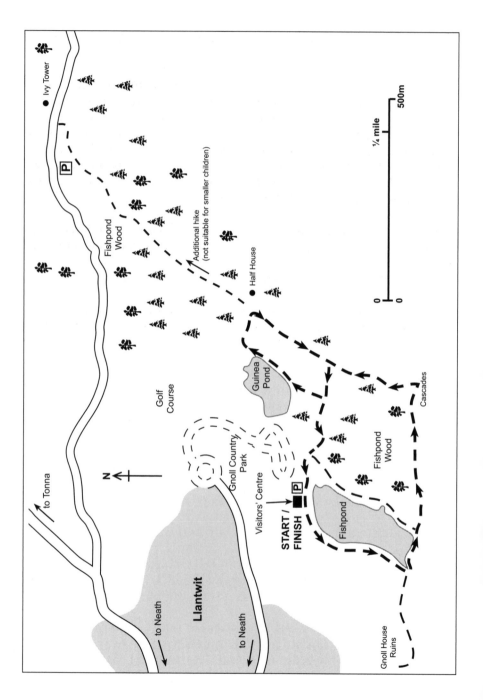

to Tonna

to Neath

Llantwit

to Neath

Gnoll Country Park

Golf Course

Visitors' Centre

START / FINISH

Fishpond

Fishpond Wood

Gnoll House Ruins

Cascades

Guinea Pond

Half House

Additional hike
(not suitable for smaller children)

Fishpond Wood

Ivy Tower

N

¼ mile

500m

interesting grotto and gazebo and flow into the Mosshouse Reservoir.

At the top of the formal cascades, the trail continues to the left on the footpath running alongside the leat, a small stream feeding the water feature. This section is level, although other paths continue uphill from here. We're in the middle of Fishpond Wood, which is full of ancient lime trees and huge beech trees and looks beautiful in the springtime, when the ground is covered with bluebells.

The French Cascades are a popular feature at the Gnoll estate

Soon the path reaches a T-junction and turns left, downhill for just a few yards before veering right and crossing the stream at the lock. Walk down to the small concrete bridge and cross to the lower path of a 'loop', with the upper path visible higher on the hillside. This area was part of Mosshouse Wood, a conifer and beech wood planted in the 1950s. Sadly the trees have been devastated by a tree disease called *Phytophthora ramorum*, which first appeared in the UK in 2002, and the landscape is now bare.

Finding the way at the Guinea Pond!

Follow the trail past the Guinea Pond, another man-made pond that had also disappeared by the time renovations began and that had to be dug out and re-lined with clay. It's now home to lots of wildlife. Shortly the trail takes a right angle and starts climbing uphill towards

The Half House is one of the Gnoll's quirky landmarks

the Half House, which was once set amongst the trees but is now plainly visible. From here walkers also get a clear view to the ruins of Ivy Tower, which was built by the Mackworths in 1795 as a viewing tower overlooking the informal cascades and was later lived in by Lucy Lewis's family.

It's possible to turn left along the level path, just below the steps to the Half House, and walk all the way through Mosshouse Wood to the hill on which the Ivy Tower stands. This links with the start of the Lucy Lewis trail, which goes to Aberdulais Tin Works and Waterfall. From here it would make an interesting hike for adults and teenagers but is too far and challenging for younger children, who will no doubt be much more interested in stopping for a while to play in the Half House! Also note that the path from here through Mosshouse Wood is made from large, loose stones and can make quite uncomfortable walking, as well as becoming muddy in poor weather.

The charming Half House is typical of the quirky features and follies the Mackworths built throughout the Gnoll estate. It now looks rather forlorn on the empty hillside but must have made a romantic hideaway when secluded amongst the trees. From the Half House, follow the upper path as it loops back in the direction of the visitor centre. As the trail starts to run downhill, with the stream now on the left, the car park and a large adventure play area can be seen ahead. This play area is ideal for older children, whilst the playground inside the main park, next to the visitor centre, is designed for younger children. The trail passes the adventure area and returns to the visitor centre and the Fishpond.

There is plenty at the Gnoll to entertain children of all ages. Older children might be interested in orienteering, which has been set up around a number of permanent control points throughout the park. Orienteering costs £1 and the maps are available from the visitor centre. There is also a nine-hole pitch and putt golf course next to the main access road, with equipment available for hire from the visitor centre for a returnable £5 deposit. Dogs are welcome in the park but should be kept on leads and under control.

WALK 17
Lucy Lewis Walks to Work, Neath

This trail follows the route taken to work each morning by tinplate worker Lucy Lewis in the 1840s. Lucy lived in the Ivy Tower on the hill overlooking the village of Tonna, and walked a mile and a half down the valley to the works and back again each day. The National Trust now runs Aberdulais Tin Works and Waterfall and many visitors have enjoyed a guided walk, led by staff and volunteers dressed in Victorian costume, following Lucy's route.

Approx. distance	1.5 miles (linear route)
Approx. time	1 hour
Starting point	Mosshouse Wood car park, Tonna
Grading	A steep and sometimes uneven walk downhill through woodland and on tarmac
Suggested age	6+
Map	OS Explorer 165

Lucy, who was 16 in 1842, lived in the Ivy Tower with her mother and her three sisters. Her father had died by the time she was working at Aberdulais. Lucy left home at 5:30am each day, working until 6pm or 7pm, and there were no street lamps to guide her journey to and from work, the only lighting coming from the huge furnaces burning further down the valley.

The trail is linear so you will have to think about the logistics of getting back to Mosshouse Wood, bearing in mind the return journey is uphill all the way! Energetic children should be able to make the climb quite easily and manage the three-mile round trip, and an

Ivy Tower

above: The ruins of the Ivy Tower, as it looks today
left: The Ivy Tower as it would have looked in Lucy's time
(*Photos courtesy of the National Trust*)

alternative is that one of the adults in your group drops everyone at the starting point and picks up at Aberdulais Tin Works and Waterfall. Note that the trail is very uneven in places and one section follows the path of a shallow creek, making wellies advisable!

Mosshouse Wood car park is at the rear of the Gnoll Estate Country Park. It's a couple of miles from the Gnoll's main car park and accessed by a different

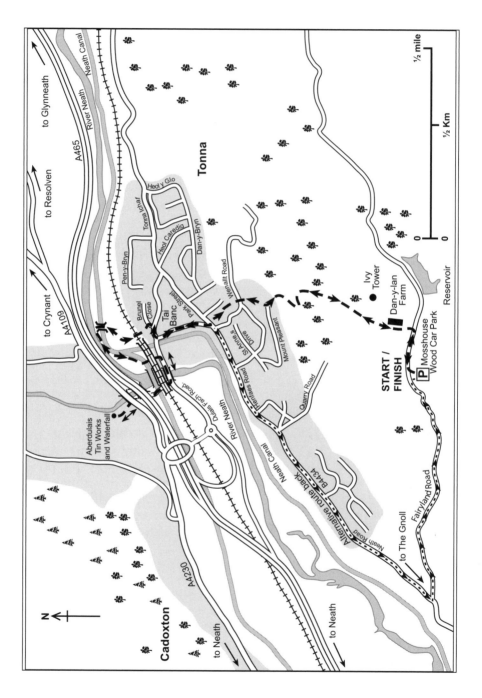

N

Cadoxton

to Neath

to Neath

A4230

Aberdulais
Tin Works
and Waterfall

to Crynant

A109

to Resolven

to Glynneath

A465

River Neath

Neath Canal

Tonna

Tonna Ichaf

Hedl y Glo

Hedl Caredig

Dan-y-Bryn

Pen-y-Bryn

Brunel
Close

Tai
Banc

Park Street

Daes Fach Road

River Neath

Wenallt Road

St Anne's
Drive

Mount Pleasant

Tennaes Road

Quarry Road

Neath Canal

Neath Road

B4434

Alternative route back

Ivy
Tower

Dan-y-Ian
Farm

START /
FINISH

P Mosshouse
Wood Car Park

Fairyland Road

to The Gnoll

Reservoir

0   ½ Km

0   ½ mile

road, so be aware of this when planning your route. To get to Mosshouse Wood, take the B4434 from Tonna towards Neath and turn left at Llantwit Cemetery, following a lane called Fairyland Road uphill for just over half a mile. The car park is on the right and the ruins of the Ivy Tower can be seen on the hill ahead.

In early 2014 the car park was closed due to an outbreak of the tree disease *Phytophthora ramorum* in the woods. It was due to reopen in March but, at the time of writing in April 2014, it remained closed. Fairyland Road is wide enough in places to park alongside the hedge, although clearly this is at your own risk.

From the car park, follow the lane uphill towards the tower. Built in 1795 by the owners of the Gnoll, it was originally named 'The Belvedere', which means a structure that has an impressive view. Guests of the Mackworths, who owned the estate, used it for refreshments when out walking and as a small ballroom! It was also once the home of the Gnoll Estate's gamekeeper. In 1920 it was destroyed by fire and is now protected by heritage group Cadw. Because of its setting, the tower appears an envious place to have lived, but the reality for Lucy and her family was probably a very cold, dark and isolated home.

There is no public access to the tower now, but the trail runs close below. Leave Fairyland Road via the metal gate at Dan y Lan Farm on the left, following the sign-posted bridleway as it runs alongside the wooden fence then cuts across the field uphill towards the tower. Go through a second gate, after which the path drops down, following the curve of the hill. Ahead are clear views across the Vale of Neath and towards Waterfall Country, which is the setting of the Waterfall Walk in Chapter 15.

Cross the farm track and climb over the wooden stile, which is a good point from which to see the town of Neath and the landmark spire of St David's Church. Follow the wide path and imagine how dark and lonely it would have been for Lucy every morning! The path reaches a woodland 'T-junction', with a blue bridleway sign pointing the way left, downhill. This is the point at which it might start to get a bit wet! The creek can be completely dry in a warm spell but, after prolonged rain, it can run a few inches deep from here on.

Shortly there are two more blue signs, one way continuing straight ahead along the wide track and the other heading right along a narrower path. Take the right path, going carefully as it's very stony and slippery in running water. The creek soon crosses another shallow stream, which diverts the water and our trail becomes a little drier from here on, although it's still stony and uneven.

A little further down, the trail reaches a road dotted with several houses. Cross the road and carry on downhill along the wide path to Wenallt Road, which is where Lucy's journey would have become better lit and she would have met other people going to work, such as miners on their way to the colliery. The colliery was important for the tinplate works as coal was needed for the furnaces and would have been brought down in trams later throughout the day.

Cross Wenallt Road and continue downhill along the path, which bears slightly to the left and is quite steep. The chimneystack of the tinplate works can be seen ahead at the bottom of the valley. Walk down to the main road, passing the Whittington Arms on the corner. Many of the terraced houses along here would have been owned by the tinplate works in Lucy's day and the road would have been busy with people setting out for work by the time Lucy reached it.

Cross the road and head towards the red former telephone box on the right, which has now been turned into an information booth. Phone boxes with a working phone inside them are a rare find now that most people have mobile phones, but in Lucy's day the phone was yet to be invented! Beyond the phone box, follow the tarmac path downhill, past the Calor Gas site below and into Tai Banc lane.

At the bottom of Tai Banc, turn right and cross the road into Brunel Close, keeping to the left pavement. You will shortly see a footpath on the left; take this and cross the bridge over the railway. Lucy wouldn't have crossed this bridge in 1842 because the Vale of Neath Railway was not built until 1851, but we can see from old maps that Upper Works employees got across the canal and the River Neath by taking a combined footbridge and dramway. Beyond the railway line, the footpath heads downhill towards the canal, following the contours of the hillside and heading towards another bridge that crosses the canal.

The canal was built more than 200 years ago, following a meeting in the Ship and Castle pub in Neath, where plans to create a canal from Pontneddfechan to Neath were first discussed. Pontneddfechan is further up the Vale of Neath and is the starting point for the Waterfall Walk in Chapter 15. A very famous engineer called Thomas Dadford was employed and the Neath Canal, at 13.5 miles long and with 19 locks, was completed in 1799.

Cross the canal bridge and, at the bottom of the steps, continue along the towpath. At the bend look left, where you'll see a stone buttress. On this spot was a wooden bridge built to allow the tin workers to cross the canal. This bridge led to a footpath and the river bridge carrying the combined footbridge and dramway.

The towpath leading to Pont Gam, or 'crooked bridge'

Ahead is a 'skew' bridge known as Pont Gam, which is Welsh for 'crooked bridge'! Skew bridges, although not common, were needed in certain circumstances to allow sufficient clearance for passing barges. Beyond the skew bridge the towpath arrives in the Aberdulais Basin, which is where the Tennant and the Neath canals meet. There also used to be a dry dock, where barges would be brought for checking and repairing.

The Tennant Canal, built by George Tennant, was intended to link the Tawe and Neath rivers. Work got underway in 1817 and the canal was complete from Swansea to Jersey Marine by 1818, but barges from the Neath Canal could not cross the river. As a result, a further extension was started to link with the Neath Canal basin at Aberdulais.

Follow the path along the right bank of the basin as it runs towards the huge arches of the railway viaduct. Before reaching the arches, take a detour to the right, onto the bank of the River Neath, where you can see the aqueduct and viaduct running parallel. The aqueduct, at 340ft long and with its 10 arches, was pretty impressive in its day, but then came the railway viaduct, which is much higher. From the bank it looms imposingly behind the smaller bridge and it's easy to see why many people saw the railways as such a threat.

Retrace your steps back to the basin, cross the canal and walk through the only accessible arch of the viaduct back to Dulais Fach Road. Head right, past the Railway Inn, stopping on the road bridge to look upriver. From here is a clear view of the viaduct and aqueduct from the other side and, interestingly, from this direction the busy A465 road bridge is also visible, reflecting transport through the ages from canal barges to trains to cars!

Over the road bridge, turn right towards the Royal British Legion and cross the canal. To the left is Canal Side, its row of cottages once owned by the tinplate works and now painted in striking colours. Follow the tarmac path as it bears right, walk under the A465 bridge and up the steps, and you've reached Aberdulais Tinworks and Waterfall!

This is one of the oldest tin works in Britain and now includes excellent displays on how tin was made and what it was used for. The displays bring characters such as Lucy to life and children might also enjoy seeing the collection of tin toys on show as well as excellent Tin Detective packs. The toys are probably very different to the toys in your homes! The site is exciting to explore, with a huge waterwheel, the chimneystack seen from the trail earlier and the foundations of buildings such as the furnace and tinning house. And, of course, there's a great viewing platform next to the falls, where the noise of the water can be pretty loud!

The National Trust charges admission to enter the tinplate works site, which contributes to the cost of essential conservation work carried out to preserve this part of our local heritage. It's also particularly good value for money and on public holidays there are usually children's activities, old-fashioned lawn games like hoopla and quoites and the chance to dress up in Victorian costume like Lucy. The tearooms and toilet block are sited just before the visitor centre entrance and are open to the public without the need to pay admission. Aberdulais Falls is a relatively small Trust property but there is plenty to do and see and I'd recommend factoring in a couple of hours for your visit.

National Trust warden Georgina Snook leads the walk

If you're making the return climb to Mosshouse Wood, an alternative route from the top of Tai Banc is along the main road (Henfaes Road becoming Neath Road) to the cemetery and turning left into Fairyland Road. It's slightly longer, extending the round trip to about three and a half miles, but the long, level stretch along the pavement is welcome relief for tired legs before the final climb for the last half-mile!

WALK 18
Village Venture, Glyncorrwg, Neath Port Talbot

This trail is called the Village Venture, but the peaceful village of Glyncorrwg is only part of the story! There's a lot more to the walk than that, as it starts and finishes at the scenic Glyncorrwg Ponds and ventures into the blissfully quiet Cwm Corrwg. But the village and its history are at the heart of this circular trail and local amenities such as the village shop and the café are handy if you need to stock up on forgotten provisions to fuel your walk!

The Village Venture is another trail in the Ramblers Cymru series created to get families out walking and exploring the local countryside. It was designed in partnership with Neath Port Talbot Council and features a countryside character called Ranger Bryn, who's said to live in Glyncorrwg. There are also questions for children to answer along the way. For more information on the packs, visit **www.ramblers.org.uk/wales** *or email* **Cerddwyr@ramblers.org.uk**.

Approx. distance	3 miles
Approx. time	1.5 hours
Starting point	Glyncorrwg Ponds, Ynyscorrwg Park, Glyncorrwg
Grading	A mainly level walk along riverside paths and through the village
Suggested age	5+
Map	OS Explorer OL12

The trail starts at Glyncorrwg Ponds visitor centre. Take the A4107 from Port Talbot to Cymmer then follow the signs to Glyncorrwg for about two miles along Heol y Glyn before reaching the ponds on the left hand side. Just a few years ago there was very little to do in the area and few jobs for local people, so residents decided to take action and establish an outdoor centre to make the most of the beautiful setting and enviable views. Glyncorrwg is within the 48-square-mile Afan Forest Park, which is known as 'little Switzerland' as its Alpine-like forestry is so picturesque. The following regeneration project between residents, the council and tourism and environmental organisations has put the Glyncorrwg countryside on the map, with people now visiting from all over the UK and abroad.

Afan Forest Park has a world-class reputation for its series of mountain bike trails. Some of these start from Glyncorrwg Ponds and the recently opened Mountain Bike Centre here is ideal for experienced mountain bikers and family cyclists alike. Bikes can be hired from the Skyline Cycles bike shop, and there's also a jet wash for cleaning muddy bikes after your trail.

Glyncorrwg Ponds are a magnet for walkers and cyclists

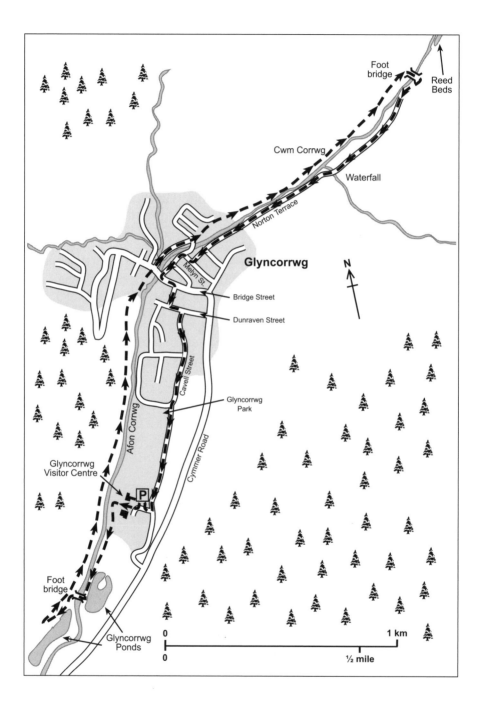

Foot
bridge
Reed
Beds
Cwm Corrwg
Waterfall
Norton Terrace
Glyncorrwg
Melyn St.
Bridge Street
Dunraven Street
Cavell Street
Glyncorrwg
Park
Cymmer Road
Afon Corrwg
Glyncorrwg
Visitor Centre
P
Foot
bridge
Glyncorrwg
Ponds
N

0   1 km
0   ½ mile

Note that there is a small charge to park at the visitor centre. From the car park, follow the path bearing left, past the Mountain Bike Centre and alongside the Afon, or River, Corrwg. Walk past the playing fields on the left to reach the ponds, keeping to the right as the path slopes downwards and avoiding the 'gate' to the left. The series of ponds is a haven for birds, animals and insects, so look out for heron, pied flycatchers and dragonflies. You might even see a kite or a buzzard overhead.

At the far end of the first pond, turn right over the long wooden bridge. Along here are several bird boxes in the trees, so look out for signs of birdlife. As the path approaches the second pond, a small clearing on the right is lined with wooden benches and is a tranquil place to rest and take in the view. There are also some interesting details to spot here, including a pretty snail mosaic set in the grass and a number of animal carvings on the benches.

The path continues right, climbing upwards. It's a steep stretch but it's the only sharp climb of the trail and it's not far, quickly reaching a tarmac path. Turn right along the path and follow it as it heads back in the direction of Glyncorrwg village, passing the visitor centre in the park below. The views from this hillside path are good and there are noticeboards along the way with information about Glyncorrwg's history.

One board says that a tithe barn used to stand here on the Dunraven estate. Tithes were the taxes of their day and workers on the estate would have to pay a proportion of their earnings in 'kind' to pay for the upkeep of the parish. For example, they would have had to hand over goods such as crops, wool or milk. It was usual for workers to contribute one tenth of what they had – which is a bit like having to give away one tenth of your pocket money every week!

The weighbridge was used to weigh out miners' quotas of coal

About half a mile along the tarmac, the trail reaches a metal

This pretty waterfall is passed on the way back to Glyncorrwg

barrier and a path leading into Glyncorrwg village. On the right is the old weighbridge, which was capable of weighing up to 12 tons! The miners who worked in the colliery were entitled to between eight and ten tons of free coal every year and this is where it was weighed out. More than 100 years ago, Glyncorrwg was a busy village with hundreds of men working underground in the colliery. The village also had lots of pubs for them to relax in after work! But the pits closed in the 1970s and many people moved away to find jobs elsewhere, leaving the village the much quieter place it is today.

Cross Bridge Street beyond the barrier and follow the lane straight ahead, between the Millennium commemorative stone and the house on the corner. The Afon Corrwg remains to the right. The trail quickly reaches another small tarmac road; cross this and follow the red way-markers along the path close to the riverbank. The trail now leaves the village behind and heads into the pretty Cwm Corrwg countryside, where the path becomes narrower and quite stony in places.

Follow the 'cwm', or valley, for half a mile, until the path forks. Bear right, downhill slightly, towards a bridge crossing the river. This is the 'head' of the trail before it doubles back towards the village on the other side of the river, and the reed bed here is an ideal place for a rest and a picnic. Reed beds are a natural filtering system, turning the dirty and polluted water from old, derelict mines into clean water.

Return towards Glyncorrwg along the path, which soon joins Norton Road and Norton Terrace. At the T-junction, turn right into Melyn Street and then left into Commercial Street. At the end of the road, we're back at Bridge Street, albeit a little further along from the place we crossed earlier. Turn left into Bridge Street and then take the first right into an unnamed lane before turning left into Dunraven Street, passing the village store on the right and the community centre on the corner. Turn right onto a tarmac lane and follow it past Glyncorrwg Park. From here it's a short distance back to the visitor centre.

This is a hub of activity for mountain bikers, walkers, fly fishers and families. As well as housing Skyline Cycles, it's well stocked with information on things to do and places to visit, and has toilets and hot showers. The first floor café has a comfy lounge area and outside decking, whilst there's even a camping and caravanning site in the grounds. And if all that walking and cycling isn't enough exercise for one day, visitors can test their fitness on the outdoor gym which, with all the fresh air, greenery and peace anyone could wish for, certainly beats a pumping, packed indoor gym, even on a crisp autumn day.

WALK 19
The Pulpit Walk, Margam Country Park, Margam

Margam Country Park was a firm family favourite when I was a child and now, with children of my own, history is repeating itself. Arguably one of the best family days out in south Wales, Margam Park has a great mix of peace and adventure, exciting activities and quiet corners from which to escape the crowd. The Pulpit Trail starts from the heart of the park but soon reaches the relative solitude of the hillside above Margam, leaving the hustle and bustle of the park below.

Approx. distance	2.5 miles
Approx. time	1.5 hours
Starting point	Margam Castle, Margam Park
Grading	A short but relatively steep climb and descent, with stony and grassy paths
Suggested age	5+
Map	OS Explorer 165

Margam Country Park sits above Port Talbot, rolling away from the steel town into untamed countryside. Its location just off the M4 makes it accessible and, importantly for cash-careful parents, it can be an inexpensive day out. Margam is owned and managed by Neath Port Talbot Council and admission to the park itself is free. There's a small charge for the car park but, other than that, visitors have a choice over the extras they wish to pay for, with many attractions included in the free admission.

Monty the narrow gauge railway engine, which runs from the car park to the castle, is popular with younger children and costs only a few pounds for a family ticket. There's also an additional charge for the Go Ape Tree-Top Adventure high ropes but many of Margam's best bits are free. This includes Fairytale Land, a imaginative outdoor village made of child-sized nursery rhyme houses, each telling a story, and a castle crammed with passageways, towers and battlements. Fairytale Land is a real treasure for under-eights whilst, for older children, there's a wooden fortress with elevated walkways, rope bridges and a towering keep.

Margam has a great deal of history, with a monastery built here during the Dark Ages. The monks who lived here were also farmers, growing crops on the land that now forms the park as well as in the fields between Cornelly and Aberafan. The ruins of Margam Abbey are in the grounds, next to the impressive 18th century orangery, which is a popular venue for weddings and other events. The monastery fell into ruins after the powerful King Henry VIII got rid of the monasteries in Wales and England, and the land was later bought by the wealthy Mansel family, who already had castles at Oxwich and Penrice in Gower.

A later branch of the family called the Mansel Talbots decided to build a new family home at Margam in the 19th century and created the Gothic-style mansion in the middle of the park. It was designed in the style of a castle, with mock battlements, turrets and a huge, octagonal tower rising from the middle. But, like many grand Victorian estates, Margam ran into financial trouble in the 20th century and the castle was already sliding into a sorry state of dereliction when its interior was destroyed by fire in 1977.

Since then, the council has carried out a lot of restoration work and, although the majority of the castle's rooms are closed to the public, visitors can walk into the vast entrance hall and peer up into the imposing staircase. Some visitors might think it's a shame that more restoration work hasn't been done but I like the sense of the castle being frozen in time, giving the park much of its character.

The Pulpit Trail starts near the castle and follows one of Margam's oldest tracks. It's said that Bronze Age people followed this route to reach the coast, whilst Roman soldiers also marched along it to their barracks in Brecon. Standing just outside the castle courtyard, with the castle on your left, follow the path towards the wooded hillside, passing Go Ape on your right. As you reach the cleft into the hills, bear left slightly. The defensive ditches of a Celtic Iron Age hill fort are visible on the left hand side. This was a relatively safe place for Celts to settle and their enclosures consisted of deep ditches with walls built of tall logs to protect themselves and their animals. From here they had far-reaching views of potential enemies on the attack.

Margam Castle
Photo courtesy of Margam Country Park

The wooded hillside is an important site for wildlife. Oak, beech and chestnut trees grow here and provide food for several species of bird, including warblers, nuthatches, treecreepers and woodpeckers. In the autumn, squirrels, deer and blackbirds and pigeons feast on the chestnuts and acorns whilst bats make their homes in many of the older trees.

Soon the trail reaches a three-pronged fork, the path you're on continuing straight ahead whilst two wind upwards to the right. Take the middle trail, way-marked in blue, and follow it up and around onto a wider path, which is quite steep and rugged in places. To start with the views are obscured by rhododendrons but the trail soon opens out onto moorland. There's a chance you'll share the scenery with the park's deer, which come this way in search of the sweet grass that grows here.

The pulpit stone looms into view on the brow of the hill ahead. The track up to pulpit and beyond, leading out of the park, is said to be

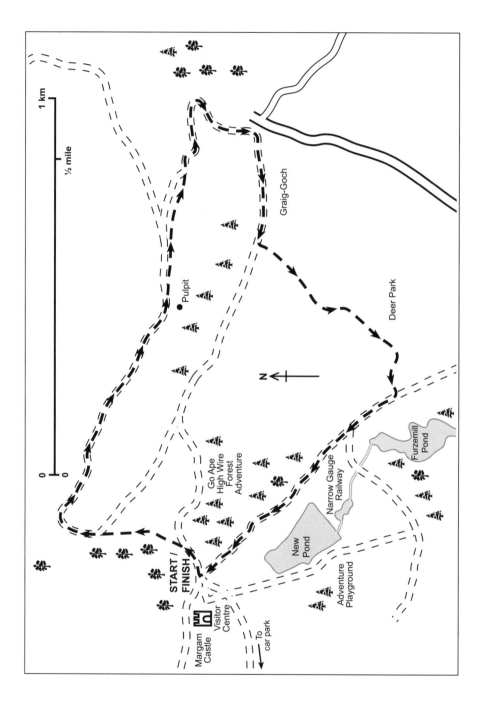

the oldest trail here, dating back to the Bronze Age. Margam's medieval monks also used it as a drove road to take their animals to market. It could be a dangerous journey, as the farmers who used this road were often waylaid by sheep and cattle thieves and bandits!

The pulpit viewpoint is marked by a large commemorative stone unveiled by Prince Charles to celebrate the work of the Prince's Trust in Wales. The stone is inscribed with 'bro', to mark the Bro Scheme, but the 'b' it looks more like a number six to many walkers! From here the views are amazing on a clear day, stretching to the Gower peninsula and north Devon. Closer is the Port Talbot skyline, dominated by the steelworks, and the Eglwys Nunydd reservoir on the other side of the M4.

The long grass around the pulpit is an excellent nesting ground for the skylark and children can have fun trying to spot the hares that live on this hillside. If you're particularly lucky you'll catch sight of a

The Pulpit's standing stone *Photo courtesy of Margam Country Park*

raven, which are drawn to Margam as its mix of open ground and woodland makes an ideal habitat for them.

From the pulpit follow the path left as it runs just below the ridge of the hill in the direction of the park's boundary wall. It soon drops to the right and descends the flank of the hill, joining a more defined, way-marked track. This valley is colourful in the springtime, filled with bluebells, foxgloves, violets and wood sorrel. You might also hear stonechats or even see a buzzard overhead.

The trail reaches the far end of the parkland and veers right. This is the heart of the deer's grazing pasture and the beautiful creatures have become synonymous with Margam, although they remain shy and adult deer, protective of their young, will be keen to keep a safe distance. Margam Country Park has the largest herd of fallow deer in south Wales, originally brought here around 600 years ago. Fallow deer are most active in the autumn, when the mating season begins and adult bucks battle for territory.

In recent years, other deer species, including red deer and Pere David deer, have been introduced to Margam. The Pere David breed originated in Peking and is rare today, only being bred in a small number of parks and zoos. Margam's boggy, rhododendron-filled land suits this breed, which has thrived since arriving here.

From the deer park, take the tarmac path back towards the castle and visitor centre, following the route of the narrow gauge railway. Between Easter

Margam Country Park is renowned
for its deer
Photo courtesy of Margam Country Park

and late September, Monty goes past several times a day and waving at the passengers is obligatory!

After your walk, there is plenty to keep you occupied for a full day out. Geocaching, a game of hiding and finding treasure, has become very popular and a number of geocache sites are concealed throughout the park. Some are close to the pathways but others are a little more challenging to find! All you need to start geocaching is a GPS device and a little knowledge about the etiquette of the activity. If you take something from a geocache box, the done thing is to replace it with something similar or of equal value. To find out more, visit **www.geocaching.com**

Families can also learn new skills on one of Margam's orienteering courses and in school holidays and on weekends there are often activities such as bushcraft, willow weaving and falconry displays. The discovery centre, which is open for day and residential visits and can be found near the animal park, has a café, and there's also a country kitchen-style tearoom in the castle's former stable block, with extra seating in the cobbled courtyard,

The Pulpit Trail is just one option from Margam's tapestry of paths and trails, which includes short, family-friendly strolls and, for hikers, a section of the arduous 36-mile Coed Morgannwg Way. As well as the farm trail through the animal park there's also an innovative Good Vibrations trail, where children can play giant wooden instruments crafted from trees felled at Margam.

Our favourite thing about Margam Country Park is that each visit is different. We never run out of new corners to explore and the parkland is equally beautiful in winter as it is in summer, its striking reds, oranges and greens at their glowing best on a crisp, cold day. The Pulpit Trail is a lovely introduction to the park but it's likely that, after your first visit, you'll keep getting drawn back and will find many trails of your own to explore.

WALK 20

The River and Railway Trail, Afan Forest Park

If you have a certain idea in your mind about 'the Valleys', it might be time to think again! The south Wales valleys often get a bad press and their stunning scenery and fascinating history can be overlooked. Yet for anyone in search of adventure, the valleys provide the perfect escape, as they are easily accessible and unexpectedly full of exciting things to do.

Approx. distance	3 miles
Approx. time	2 hours
Starting point	Afan Forest Park Visitor Centre, Afan Valley
Grading	A mainly level forestry walk with some steep and uneven climbs
Suggested age	5+
Map	OS Explorer 165

The Afan Valley above the steel town of Port Talbot is one of the narrowest valleys in south Wales and arguably the most beautiful. Whereas the valleys further east are characterised by grassy, rolling hills and the visible scars of their mining heritage, the Afan Valley is marked by dense forestry and renowned for its Alpine-like appearance.

The area is so good for walking it was made a forest park more than 40 years ago and the criss-crossing trails are now popular with walkers and cyclists alike. Trails start from many points along the valley but the busiest hub is the Afan Forest Park visitor centre. Note that the park used to be called Afan Argoed Country Park and is still known as this locally, so if you're asking for directions you might get sent to 'Afan Argoed'!

The main car park can fill up early with cars, vans and bike trailers and there can be so much coming and going that you do need to keep an extra eye on small children whilst you're preparing to set off. The charge to park is £1. The visitor centre itself is a lively place, housing not only the Trailhead Café and a packed information centre but also a bike hire point and the South Wales Miners' Museum, which is well worth the small, additional admission fee.

The visitor centre's foyer is also the place to pick up activity sheets. You might want to try the nature quiz or have a go at Bingo in the Park, which is a fun way of spotting along your walk sights such as water lilies, brambles, ducks, swans and even joggers! The Use Your Senses sheet allows even more imagination, as players have to help a short-sighted mole find non-specific items such as 'something tiny'

History on display at Afan Forest Park visitor centre

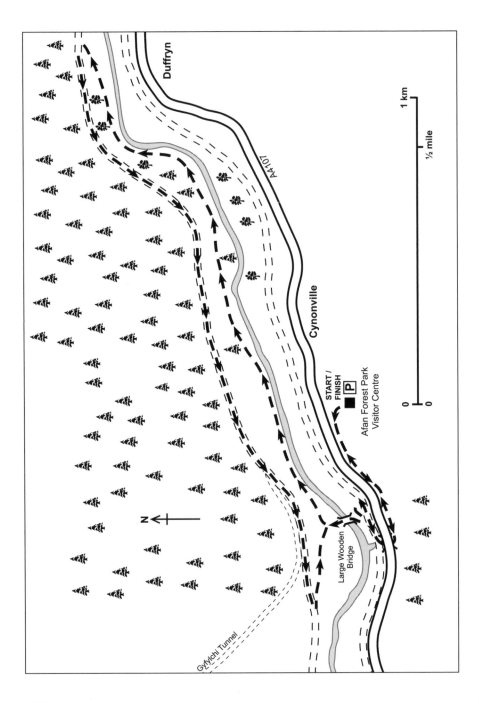

Duffryn

A4107

Cynonville

START /
FINISH
P
Afan Forest Park
Visitor Centre

Large Wooden
Bridge

Gyfylchi Tunnel

N

0   ½ mile   1 km

and 'something moving fast'. The sheets are available in English and Welsh.

The River and Railway Trail is one of several starting from the visitor centre. The trails range widely in distance and difficulty, with this one being amongst the intermediate options. It's mainly level but does have some sections that would prove tricky with pushchairs, although it's ideal for walkers with baby carriers.

Follow the yellow railings to the left of the visitor centre (as you stand with your back to the building) and cross the small wooden bridge. The Afan Valley has fallen victim to the same tree disease that has affected some of the Neath trails also included in this book, and many of the trees in this area had been felled at the time of writing.

Head down the slope to the road bridge and pass underneath to the other side, which is the starting point for several trails. It's also the path of the Afan Valley Cycleway, a National Cycle Network linking the head of the valley with Aberavon seafront. The River and Railway Trail is way-marked from here in orange.

Cross the cycle path and walk downhill on the zig-zag path. Cyclists are supposed to dismount on this steep section but not all do, so watch out as some might approach at speed. At the riverbank, follow the path right, looking out for the large commemorative stone just before the bridge. This marks the route of the Coed Morgannwg Way, which is a 36-mile trail between Merthyr Tydfil and Margam Park. That's the equivalent of walking this trail 12 times!

Cross the River Afan (or Afon Afan in Welsh, which is not too easy to say!) at the large wooden bridge. In this area was the old road to Neath, and a blacksmith's forge was built here more than 300 years ago. The trail continues past a meadow with picnic tables then it forks as it reaches the trees. Follow the right fork, along the riverbank; the path on the left is the way the trail returns later.

The riverside path is a peaceful section that doesn't get too crowded and enjoys the shade of the trees. The path runs uphill ever so slightly and at points moves further from the river, but the water remains within earshot if not always in sight and the trail soon drifts back

The trail follows the River Afan

towards it. Every now and again, cycle routes merge from the left and at one point a well-defined fork appears; each time stay right, continuing roughly parallel with the river.

Eventually the track narrows into a footpath requiring single file. Soon the orange markers point upwards via a few 'steps' with a small wooden railing and the trail leads away from the river, becoming very steep. It's hard going but before long a flight of wooden steps brings the path to a clearing and the forest road, with a handy picnic area for those in need of a breather after the climb!

The road was once the South Wales Mineral Railway, built by a famous engineer called Isambard Kingdom Brunel to take coal from Glyncorrwg to Briton Ferry Docks. Follow the road left, returning in the direction of the visitor centre but now high above the river. There are great views across the valley to Cynonville from this level.

The forest might seem as though it's been here for ever but, in fact, the mountainside was once covered with oak woodland. But the copper and tinplate works which sprang up in Swansea and Neath in the 19th century needed timber, so the oak trees were cut down and transported to the works. In the 1930s, the planting of the forest began and Afan Forest Park now makes up part of the biggest urban forest in western Europe.

Whilst walking along the forest road, keep a look-out for birds of prey, such as buzzards, flying above. The park is home to many birds, including willow warblers, chiff-chaffs, pied flycatchers and ravens, and more information about the park's wildlife can be found in the visitor centre.

After about half a mile, a stony track forks from the road at a slight gradient. This is the route to take if you want to see the remains of the Gyfylchi tunnel, a 1109-yard tunnel designed by Brunel to carry the mineral railway through the mountain. The track is very rough and the half-mile to the tunnel makes for uncomfortable walking, so families with small children might instead prefer to stick to the main forest road until reaching a narrow footpath in the bank to the right and making the short, sharp climb to the tunnel.

There is not much of the tunnel to see now as the entrance has long been closed up, although history and rail buffs will think it worth the extra climb. It was closed in 1947, having been used to store ammunition during World War II.

From the tunnel, return down the bankside to the forest road and continue for a short distance. Don't go down the narrow paved path to the left but

The forest road used to be a mineral railway

instead walk a little further on and take a second, wider path down, which doubles back from the forest road and returns to the meadow.

From here, cross the wooden bridge and climb back up to the visitor centre. On reaching the level of the centre, look back across the valley and try to spot the Gyfylchi tunnel. You can see from here how far you've walked!

Alternative trails for families in Afan Forest Park include The Old Parish Road Walk, an easy 1.25m stroll along the old Rhondda and Swansea Bay Railway Line from the visitor centre, and the Rhyslyn Trail, a mainly flat 2.5m route starting further down the valley at Pontrhydyfen. At the time of writing, some of Afan's trails were closed for maintenance; they were due to reopen later in 2014 but it might be wise to phone ahead of your visit to check which routes are accessible.

Beamer tramper electric buggies are available to hire from the visitor centre and many events and activities are run throughout the year, including food festivals and bat watching. If you have time to explore more of the Afan Forest Park, don't miss the Kanji Wood near Pontrhydyfen. The park was twinned with the Nagano Prefecture area of Japan in 2003 and, to celebrate, Port Talbot's Japanese community helped to design the Kanji woodland garden. The wood consists of many species of tree, including conifers, broadleaf and Japanese plants, and has a number of sculptures featuring Kanji, a form of Japanese writing.

Glyncorrwg Ponds are another highlight for walkers and cyclists. The forest park is regularly named one of the UK's 'must visit' areas by mountain biking magazines and several trails start from Glyncorrwg Ponds Visitor Centre, where bikes can also be hired. See Chapter 18 for more information on things to do there and for the Village Venture trail.